𝕿𝖍𝖊 𝕾𝖆𝖎𝖓𝖙𝖘 𝖆𝖓𝖉 𝕾𝖊𝖗𝖛𝖆𝖓𝖙𝖘 𝖔𝖋 𝕲𝖔𝖉.

THE LIFE

OF THE BLESSED

MARY ANN OF JESUS,

DE PAREDES Y FLORES,

AN AMERICAN VIRGIN.

CALLED

THE LILY OF QUITO.

BY FATHER JOSEPH BOERO, S. J.

PHILADELPHIA:

PUBLISHED BY PETER F. CUNNINGHAM,
104 SOUTH THIRD STREET.
M.D.CCC.LV.

A. M. D. G.

TO THE LADIES OF ST. ROSE'S SODALITY ATTACHED TO ST. JOSEPH'S CHURCH, PHILADELPHIA, PA.

AWARE of your distinguished piety, I think myself justified in presenting to your Sacred Association a translation of the life of the Blessed Mary Ann of Jesus, lately raised to the honours of the altar by his Holiness Pope Pius IX. But when I reflect also that the Blessed Rose of Lima is one of your principal patronesses, I consider myself bound to offer to your veneration another flower of South America, her near relative, the Lily of Quito.

Accept, therefore, this tribute of my sincere regard for you, and emulate the virtues of which she was so distinguished a model.

A. L. M.

Feast of St. Aloysius, 1855.

PREFACE.

To an age so corrupt and vitiated as the present, so fascinated with the pleasures, the delights and ease of the present life, and on that account an enemy of the cross of Christ and Christian penance, the life of the Blessed Mary Ann of Jesus de Paredes, lately raised to the honours of the altar by the Sovereign Pontiff Pius IX., cannot be an acceptable or an agreeable offering.

Born of a noble family and enriched with all those qualities and prerogatives which young ladies of the world so highly prize, and which they are so fond of displaying, she began from her tender years to entertain a contempt of herself, and to despise whatever the world loves and embraces; afterwards to mortify her passions and macerate her innocent flesh, making use of a thousand stratagems and ingenious inventions in her penitential course. If the facts, which are recorded, had not been juridically deposed in the different processes by a great number of eye-witnesses and persons who could be relied upon, we should scarcely be able to persuade ourselves that a little girl of a few

years, of a delicate constitution, and living in
the midst of the world, would have had the courage to undergo such an enormous amount of
rigid austerities, the recital of which alone makes
the blood creep and shudder in our veins. And
what still more increases the wonder is that she
had done nothing which deserved chastisement,
having carried her virginal purity unspotted,
and her baptismal innocence untarnished to the
grave. To say much in a few words, she was
the counterpart of St. Aloysius de Gonzaga,
whose virtues she copied and whose example
she imitated, but whom she surpassed in the
rigour of her extraordinary penances, dying also
like him in the flower of her age, in her twenty-
sixth year.

The world, engrossed with the things of the
earth, far from admiring and extolling such virtue, abominates and despises it, or at least regards it as obsolete and antiquated, and unsuited
to the carnal refinement of the age. Many also
even of the professed followers of Christ will
stare when they view such perfection and become disheartened, and despairing of ever reaching such an eminence, they will remain in their
tepidity without advancing a step.

God, however, has his own ends in view in
proposing to us these sublime and heroic examples of sanctity. In the first place he wishes to
make us see the power of his grace, which not
only renders possible but easy and agreeable
whatever is contrary to the weakness of nature.
In the second place he intends to rouse the sinner, to call him to penance, and conduct him to
the observance of the divine precepts, setting
before him certain privileged souls, enabled by
him to suffer great things, even beyond what is
needful and what he himself commands. Finally.
he gives vigour and alacrity to fervent Christians, in order that they may emulate the generous sacrifices of his dearer and more faithful
servants, if not entirely at least partially.

Such I hope will be the fruit which the well-
disposed faithful will reap from the perusal of
this life. And what gives me confidence is the
lively instances of many to have a second edition:
the first, which was issued on the occasion of the
solemn beatification, having been almost entirely
exhausted. Thanks to God, I know that it has
been read with admiration and pleasure, and
that in several souls it has produced the salutary
effects of a change of life, and an increase in

fervour. This is a sign that faith is not entirely
extinct in the hearts of Christians, and that the
actions of the just, although arduous and sublime, are strong inducements to virtue.

It was my intention to have re-published the
same history which had been distributed at the
time of the beatification, and written with no
ordinary simplicity and elegance by the pious
priest D. Giovanni del Castiglio, after having
put it, however, in somewhat better order, and
curtailed the frequent repetition, which must
have been tiresome to the reader. But when I
had set about the work and made some progress,
I found that in place of digesting it into a better
order, I had composed almost a new work.
Wherefore I no longer closely followed the
above writer, but sought to add several facts
which I had read in the process, that had been
omitted by the other, and which were well
worthy of being known.

Whatever may have been my success in this
labour, I shall consider myself as sufficiently
rewarded, and shall be perfectly satisfied, if it
redound in any measure to the glory of the
Blessed Mary Ann of Jesus, and to the spiritual
advantage of souls.

CONTENTS.

CHAPTER VI.

CHAPTER VII.

CHAPTER VIII.

CHAPTER IX.

CHAPTER X.

CHAPTER XVI.

CHAPTER XVII.

CHAPTER XVIII.

CHAPTER XIX.

CHAPTER XX.

CHAPTER XXI.

LIFE

OF THE BLESSED

MARY ANN OF JESUS,

DE PAREDES Y FLORES.

CHAPTER I.

RESEMBLANCE BETWEEN THE SANCTITY OF ST. ROSE OF LIMA AND THE BLESSED MARY ANN OF JESUS. WONDERFUL THINGS THAT TOOK PLACE BEFORE AND AFTER THE BIRTH OF MARY ANN. EXTRAORDINARY EXAMPLES OF ABSTINENCE AND CHARITY GIVEN IN HER CHILDHOOD.

For the purpose of manifesting the force of his divine grace and to enliven the fervor of faith among the inhabitants of South America, whether natives or strangers who came there from Europe, or for the benefit of those who had lately passed from idolatry to the Catholic Religion, it pleased Almighty God at the commencement of the seventeenth century to place before the world two renowned examples of extraordinary perfection and holiness. And that they might have the greater efficacy to per-

2 13

suade and move, he selected two virgins, feeble
with respect to sex, of a tender age and of very
weak constitutions. These were Rose of St.
Mary and Mary Ann of Jesus; the one born in
Lima and the other in Quito. Both having
been distinguished from their very infancy with
the clearest evidences of the divine predilection, the first received the name of *Rose*, because she was scarcely born, when the figure
and color of her face in the cradle seemed in
some measure to resemble a beautiful rose; the
second was called the Lily, from the fact that a
most odoriferous lily sprung from her blood
which continued for a long time without any
sign of corruption. Both of them lived in the
world, and after the example of St. Catherine
of Sienna, whom they both proposed to imitate,
bound themselves to God by the vows of chastity, poverty and obedience, and found their retreat and solitude within the walls of their paternal homes. They afflicted and macerated
their bodies in so many different and unusual
ways, by penances the most extraordinary, that
in this they are more worthy of admiration than
imitation. Both were virgins of angelic purity, both preserved their baptismal innocence

to their last breath, reached in a short time the
highest point of perfection and died in the
flower of their age, Rose in her 31st and Mary
Ann in her 26th year. I will say moreover,
that if the ancient traditions do not deceive us,
both had their origin from the same stock of the
family of Flores, whose surname both bore, and
hence they were related to each other by ties of
blood and a common descent from the same ancestors. Because there is a current report, that
three brothers by the name of Flores from the
city of Toledo crossed over to America from
New Spain, and that one of them settled in
Cuzco, another in Lima and a third who was
Don Girolamo Flores de Paredes, father of Mary Ann and perhaps the youngest of the three,
in Quito. Be this as it may, it is certain that
Mary Ann bore a most striking likeness to Rose
in her manner of life and her admirable sanctity ; and it would seem that God wished to per-
petuate in her, if the expression be allowed, the
copy of the other, for the latter was born not
more than a year after the death of the former.
Of all which things the reader will be better
able to judge from the facts, which will be related in this history of her wonderful life, which

with the divine assistance I have undertaken to write.

Mary Ann the subject of our memoir was born in the city of Quito on the 31st of October in the year of our Lord 1618, of Don Girolamo Flores Zenel de Paredes, a nobleman of Toledo and D. Marianna Cranobles di Xaramilo, a descendent also of one of the most illustrious Spanish families of that Kingdom. To the nobility of blood which they inherited from their ancestors, her parents united so much devotion and Christian piety, that they were a mirror and a model to their fellow citizens, who were accustomed to call the house of Paredes by no other name than *the house of prayer, and the house of saints.* Seven children, three boys and four girls were already the fruit of their holy marriage, when D. Marianna already somewhat advanced in years, perceiving herself again pregnant, was troubled with much anguish and anxiety, believing that her near confinement would prove fatal to her. But she soon had reason to lay aside all fear. A little before the middle of the night of the 31st of October being seized with the pains of labor and in great suffering, one of the servants of

the house went out into the open air, and raising her eyes to heaven ¡as if about to recommend her mistress to God, saw a most
beautiful palm formed of the brightest stars,
the trunk of which seemed to rest directly over
the room where the sick woman lay. Not being
able from stupor to articulate a single word, by
signs and gestures she called the domestics, who
ran immediately to her and among them came the
father D. Girolamo. All plainly saw it with
their eyes, and some who survived, testified in
the juridical process to this unusual and marvellous sign given by Almighty God at the birth
of this beloved little child. At that very moment D. Marianna was happily delivered, and at
the same time that wonderful group of stars
grew dim and disappeared.

The child just born appeared so amiable and
so dear on account of its beautiful features,
that it attracted the eyes and hearts of all that
were present. D. Girolama her eldest sister
took it up in her arms, and moved by feelings
of mingled delight and piety exclaimed, Alas!
O beautiful and charming infant, what have you
come to do in this miserable world! God
knows how many dangers, and what misery your

2*

beauty will bring upon you! But in this she
was certainly mistaken; and had afterwards
more than any other, cause to admire the consummate sanctity of her sister. The next day,
which was the solemnity of all saints, they
wished to have the child immediately baptized;
but all things not being yet prepared as the
father D. Girolamo wished them, it was deferred
to the 22d of November, a day sacred to the an-
nual commemoration of St. Cecilia virgin and
martyr. Her relative D. Gabriele Melendes
Granobles stood sponsor at the sacred font, and
to please the mother they gave her the name of
Mary Ann.

God having now taken possession of this
soul, filled it with the treasures of his grace,
and from that moment began to prepare her for
that lofty perfection in a wonderful manner, to
which from all eternity he had destined her.
Two things and both of them really astonishing
are related of Mary Ann's infancy; and precisely regard those two singular virtues, innocence and penance, which she afterwards cultivated, as we will see, with so much care during
the whole course of her life. D. Tommeso de
Paredes, brother of the saint, deposed in the ju-

ridical process, that the mother wishing to apply the child to her breast to suckle it, the
child at other times the most quiet and docile
of creatures indignantly refused to take any
nourishment. It passed therefore the whole of
the first day after its birth fasting, and only
towards evening it took some refreshment by
applying once to the mother's breast, and then
it would taste no more till the middle of the
next day. The very same thing happened two
or three times in succession; nor could the
mother with all her endeavors ever induce the
dear little babe to take nourishment more than
twice a day and at determinate hours, viz.
towards mid-day and about midnight. Therefore
suspecting that her own milk was tainted from
some cause, and that this made it disgusting to
her daughter, she consigned her to the nurse.
But it was all to no purpose; for the child persevered in its own way; and is was observed
moreover that on Mondays, Wednesdays and
Fridays of every week it commenced and always continued to take nourishment but once
and that at mid-day. Then at last they perceived that it was not an effect of the badness
of the nourishment, but the virtue of abstinence

which operated unpremeditatedly and as it were by a prodigy in this soul.

Nor was her love of purity, which she mani-fested from the very first days after her birth, less astonishing. Being still in her swaddling clothes everytime the servants, carrying her in their arms, went forth upon the public street, the little child showed her repugnance to ap-pear in public with her face uncovered. Where-fore as soon as she perceived that she was out of the house, she burst into a flood of tears; nor was there any way of quieting her, for the experiment was tried more than once, except by spreading over her a veil that would completely cover her and hide her from the eyes of others. So shy of the world did this child show herself and so jealous of her innocence.

These were without doubt unconscious emo-tions of grace; but signs sufficiently clear, that God in a particular manner watched over the concerns of this beloved soul. And we have in proof of it another fact which is deposed on the testimony of an eye-witness in the juridical process. A few months had hardly passed after the death of Mary Ann, when her father D. Gir-olamo passed from this to a better life in those sentiments of great piety, in which he had always lived. The widowed mother after having paid to her consort the last honours, in order to moderate a little her bitter grief, resolved to go and pass some time at one of her villas, situated in the delightful valley of Cayambe, not very far from Quito. She started therefore from the city, accompanied by her domestics, and rode a mule with her little child resting upon her bosom. Half way upon her journey she had to cross a rivulet that was much swollen by the late rain. She feared on this account to go before; but taking courage from her servants, she urged on her mule and entered the water. She had hardly advanced a few steps before the animal stumbled against a rock and bending unexpectedly forward gave the lady such a violent shock, that without perceiving it she let go the child which fell plump into the water. The terrified mother immediately uttered a piercing cry, believing for certain that her child was already strangled and carried away by the torrent. But looking down, she saw that so far from being drowned she was standing erect and firm, supported by an invisible hand. As soon as her major-domo heard of the accident, he immediately threw himself into the water, and taking the little creature, and carrying her to the opposite shore, replaced her in the arms of her mother; whose astonishment was redoubled, for pressing the child to her bosom and minutely examining her, she discovered, that not only her clothes were not wet, but not even the little shoes with which she had seen her standing upon the water.

All these singular evidences of heaven that happened before and after Mary Ann's birth, made her relations conceive the highest hopes of her. All predicted great things of her, and they began from that time to regard her with a certain reverence and more as a thing of God than of the world. The mother in particular, who was a most pious lady, took the greatest care of her and could hardly suffer her to be out of her sight. And when it happened she was obliged from necessity to entrust her for a short time to one of her sisters, she earnestly recommended to them to be extremely cautious for fear of scandalizing that angelic soul Mary Ann, because in her was reared a great servant of God.

Scarcely was she able to stand upon her feet

and to lisp, than her first words were to invoke
with tenderness the names of Jesus and Mary,
and her first acts were examples of fervour and
purity. Being one day led by the hand out of
the house by her sisters, D. Martino della Pegna met them and stopping for a moment to speak
with them, when he was on the point of taking
leave he happened to cast his eyes down upon
the little Mary Ann, who was then only two or
three years of age, and began to caress and
play with her, after which taking her up in his
arms he made pretences that he wanted to kiss
her. The little child so forcibly resented this
act of innocent freedom, and blushing from
modesty gave vent to such a flood of bitter
tears, and at the same time defended herself so
well with her puny little hands, that the doctor
struck with astonishment, as he afterwards testified in the juridical process, handed her back
immediately to her sisters without kissing her.
As to her fervour and devotion, we have the relation of a most charming little incident which
took place when she was about three years of
age. Her pious mother was in the habit of
rising in the middle of the night, and placing
herself upon her knees to pray with her arms

extended in the form of a cross. Once it happened that Mary Ann being awake gently raised the curtain with her hand, and she had no sooner seen her mother in that humble posture, than she quietly also got out of bed and placed herself on her knees at her side, and with her arms extended. Here arose a charming contest between the little child and its mother. The one insisted that the other should return to bed and sleep. The other begged to be permitted to imitate her example. In the end the child conquered, and remained a good while praying the best way it knew how, and presenting a spectacle of piety and devotion worthy the eyes of angels.

When she was weaned she omitted nothing of her abstinence, on the contrary she increased it: and moved by the interior spirit which guided her began to fast so rigorously that she frequently fainted from loss of strength and fell into mortal swoons. The mother and servants of the house, who were aware of the cause, tried every means to induce to abate something of that rigour, which it was not possible for a little child of only four years to withstand, who required food to subsist and grow. But they tried in vain: for even the little presents of fruits and sweet meats, which are so much coveted at that age, although Mary Ann received them with seeming gladness, nevertheless they were hardly received before she gave them to an Indian servant without once tasting them.

Among the other virtues that shone forth in Mary Ann still quite young was a great love towards the poor. Being informed one day that several poor persons were standing at the door expecting to get some alms, she quickly ran to her mother to get something with which to relieve them. The good lady told her that their supply of bread had not yet been brought to the house and that she had nothing that morning to give to the poor: that there was only one cake in the pantry, which she had to keep for her aged father, who would soon be there. The little child remained disconsalate, and her heart not suffering her to dismiss these poor creatures without some relief, moved by compassion and pity she began to weep. Her mother softened at the sight called her to her, and breaking the cake into pieces, gave it to her to distribute them with her own hands to the poor. She did it with a good grace and evident signs of joy:

then returning to her mother she told her not to
be uneasy, because God would without fail, pro-
vide bread for her aged parent. And in fact,
she had hardly uttered the words, before an Indian servant with a little boy, whom they had
never seen, presented themselves at the door of
the house, and in the name of a certain person,
who was also unknown, brought as a present
two baskets of the whitest bread. With all
their industry they could never discover whence
they came, or by whom they had been sent.
Only the little Mary Ann with childlike simplicity, and full of joy said—See, mamma dear,
how God has quickly sent a great supply of
bread for the cake given to the poor. Her relations were astonished at such sense in a little
child, that had scarcely begun to walk and
speak ; and they gave a thousand thanks to the
Lord, who was pleased to remunerate an alms
with so agreeable a prodigy.

In this manner she went on increasing, beloved of God and man, when all on a sudden
she lost her mother, who not long after her return from the villa to the city was called by
God to enjoy in heaven, the reward of those
christian virtues, which had rendered her an ob-

ject of admiration to the noble ladies of Quito.
Mary Ann was very much grieved, having lost
in her not only a wise and kind mother, but
also an example of perfection and sanctity. But
God soon consoled her by giving her in charge
to her eldest sister D. Girolama, who more than
any other inherited many of the qualities and
the virtues of their mother.

CHAPTER II.

HER FIRST FERVOUR IN DEVOTION AND PIETY.
SHE IS MIRACULOUSLY PRESERVED FROM MANY
DANGERS WHICH THREATENED HER LIFE. MOST
EXTRAORDINARY ARTIFICES TO AFFLICT AND
TORTURE HER INNOCENT BODY.

THE Blessed Mary Ann was in her fifth year,
when having lost her father and mother, she
went to live at the house of her sister D. Girolama, who was married to captain D. Cosimo di
Casso. This sister had three little daughters
Maria, Giovanna, and Sebastiana, with whom
she associated her little sister to be brought up

She provided them with excellent masters and mistresses, who instructed them in those arts and accomplishments, which were befitting their noble condition. Mary Ann was so assiduous and diligent, that leaving her nieces far behind, in a short time she learnt to read, write, to play on different instruments, and to sing with considerable grace and elegance. True it is, that her songs were always sacred and devout airs, and she drew from them not only pleasure and delight, but such advantage to her soul, that even in her more mature years, and when she was leading a life entirely separated from the world, she was wont, not unfrequently, to raise her mind to God by means of song. And two witnesses among the others, declared upon oath in the juridical process, that Mary Ann at different times was audibly accompanied in her songs by the angels, and that different little birds flying above her window assisted her with their sweet warbling, to praise their common Creator.

She spent all the time, which was not employed in these innocent occupations in exercises of piety : retiring to places set apart for prayer, reading good books and the Lives of Saints, and in vocal prayers. She erected a lit-

tle altar in her chamber and upon it placed a
little statue in bass-relief of the most Blessed
Virgin and another likewise of the Infant Jesus. Here she passed many hours, either in
adorning the two images, or in praying before
them; to which moreover she presented whatever little dainty was given her as a present to
eat, mortifying in this manner her appetite to
do honour to Jesus and Mary. She, although
she was younger than her three nieces, still by
her wisdom and maturity beyond her age, had
acquired such authority and reverence, that
they all regarded her as their guide and mistress. Of this she availed herself to arouse
within them the same devotion that burnt in
herself. She would gather together the little
girls of the neighbourhood who were as innocent
as herself, and in company with her three nieces
station them before the little altar, and in two
choirs make them recite the rosary and sing the
litanies. She then celebrated all the Sundays
with greater pomp and show, and especially the
festivals of our Lord and the Queen of heaven.
On the preceding vigil she prepared her companions, then all the next day she occupied
them in devout prayers, and a little before it

grew dark she closed the festival with a procession, singing pious hymns whilst they carried by turn the two images of the divine Infant and his Blessed Mother.

God was pleased to manifest by a wonderful prodigy how pleasing to him were these pious diversions of the little children. On a certain festival of the Blessed Virgin, Mary Ann had invited all the ladies belonging to the house of Paredes, and other distinguished ones of the city, who came very willingly, attracted by the piety of these little innocent creatures. Now whilst she was, according to custom, arranging the procession, it happened that a candle bending set fire to a very fine rose-coloured veil, with which Mary Ann had dressed the statue. As soon as the flames broke forth, all the ladies who were present uttered a piercing cry: and Mary Ann being made aware of the accident, immediately ran thither, and with an intrepidity more than childish, extended her hands to the burning veil, and raising it quietly from the statue, stretched it out to see where it was burnt. But to the great surprise of all it was found perfectly whole and without the smallest injury.

Another time, after having fatigued herself
the whole day with her pious occupations, the
little girl being overcome by drowsiness, gently
fell asleep. After a short time she awoke, fixed
her eyes aloft, and as if surprised between wonder and joy, quickly called to her companions
to run and see the three bright stars, which she
saw glittering over her head : be quick said
she, and awake; because it is not right that you
should be sleeping, whilst my spouse keeps
watch to do me favours. Her companions came
immediately, and placed themselves at her side,
but they saw nothing. Mary Ann insisted that
they should look with more attention ; and they
were grieved that it was not permitted them to
enjoy that pleasing sight. They were however
at that moment seized by a pleasing sense of
devotion, which filled their souls with delight.
They afterwards asked Mary Ann, what was the
meaning of the appearance of these three stars.
To whom with ingenuous candour she briefly replied ; I think notwithstanding my misery the
most august Trinity has chosen me to be his
temple.

This event being divulged abroad, many took
occasion from it to call Mary Ann *the child of*

the star: and they became more and more
grounded in the opinion already conceived, that
she was destined to great things for the honour
of God.   In this opinion they were not a little
confirmed afterward, seeing the singular protection of heaven, by which she twice escaped by
miracle from evident danger of death.   The little girls had one day ascended to the top-story
of the house, in which D. Cosimo had caused a
new floor to be laid.   Whilst they were amusing
themselves running along the scaffolding, Mary
Ann was either thoughtlessly pushed by her
companions, or approaching too near the edge
and missing her step, was precipitated from the
highest part of the building and fell upon a
heap of rubbish and stones, which were piled
up against the wall.   At the heart-rending
shriek of the little girls D. Cosimo went immediately around, and learning the accident, hurried down into the street, expecting for certain
to find his little relative not only dead, but
crushed and mashed.   But he had hardly
reached the door, when whom should he see approaching him but Mary Ann, full of joy and
smiling, and without any hurt at all.   He was
perfectly astonished; and could attribute the

fact to nothing else than to the protection of
the angels, who had supported the saint in her
perilous fall.

From another imminent risk she was timely
preserved by an interior light infused into her
mind by Almighty God. The servant of God
having noticed, that in the public processions
that were accustomed to be made in Holy Week,
there were several persons, who in the garb of
penance carried heavy crosses upon their shoulders, was inflamed with the desire of imitating
them; for this purpose she called her nieces to
her and earnestly exhorted them to endeavor
to procure also three instruments of penance
and adopt them in their domestic procession.
And as a word from her was sufficient, they immediately agreed to the proposal. But they
had no crosses; and Mary Ann undertook the
task of providing them. She collected as many
pieces of wood as were necessary, and not to be
disturbed by any one, led her companions into a
court-yard at some distance from the house to
construct the crosses. And they were all busily
engaged in this pious work, when the Blessed
servant of God suddenly rose from her work,
and in a great hurry called her nieces to follow

her. And because they were slow in moving,
she ran to where they were, and taking them by
the hand anxiously led them to the other side
of the yard. Then, all being now safe, a high
wall fell with a terrible crash upon the very
spot where the children had been at work, and
which would without doubt have crushed them,
had they not been timely removed. Mary Ann
herself, although then quite young, at the very
thought of the great risk she had run with her
companions, burst into a flood of tender tears
and gave most humble thanks to God, offering
him in all sincerity and affection her own life
in exchange, which he had already three times
given her, by preserving it by miracle from
death.

And in fact, from that time forward that she
regarded herself in no other light than as a victim offered to Jesus, I can give no better proof,
than by relating the excessively sharp and extraordinary penances, which she began to practice even at the tender age of six to seven, and
which she afterwards increased without measure, as we shall see in the course of this history.
She felt herself all inflamed with divine love,
and sensibly excited to maltreat her innocent

body to resemble more closely her afflicted
spouse Jesus, as she was always accustomed to
call him. Happening to be present one day in
the church at a funeral oration, which was pronounced in praise of a Religious, who had died
in the odour of sanctity, a lady and relative of
Mary Ann, having heard the wonderful austerity practiced during the life of the deceased, O
who could, she exclaimed, imitate this servant
of God! To whom the Blessed Mary Ann who
sat at her side, with a gravity beyond her years,
replied—with God's help love can do all. Thus,
without being aware of it, she assigned the
cause, from which she drew all her force and
strength to go forward in her austere life. Besides, it is necessary here first of all to inform
the reader, that God, always admirable in his
saints, was pleased to guide this his beloved
servant by ways quite extraordinary and out of
the usual course; and hence he would be very
much mistaken, who would wish to regard them
with a human eye and judge them only by the
rules of human prudence. The life of this
blessed servant of God was one continued prodigy of divine grace; a very rare one, and,
when we take into consideration all the circum-

stances of age, condition, sex, perhaps the only one of its kind to be found in the annals of the church. This being promised, let us come to the recital of facts.

Mary Ann had fastened around their rooms fourteen crosses, before which she and her nieces were accustomed every Friday to perform the *Stations of the cross.* She marched before carrying upon her shoulders a heavy cross of wood, and with the soles of her shoes lined with hard peas. Every one can easily imagine how painful this journey, which was by no means short, must have been to a little child, and which she performed with great slowness, passing from one room to another, and stopping at every station. Suffice it to say that not unfrequently it happened, that tormented by the pain of her feet and oppressed by the weight of the cross she would fall helpless to the ground with evident danger of being seriously hurt or injured. At other times she would cause the cross to be brought to her by her companions, and in receiving it from their hands, salute it with the most tender expressions of affection, and then dragging herself along on her bare knees with that weight upon her shoul-

ders, visit one by one the stations of the *via
crucis*. We know that the skin of her knees
was torn and that she left behind her, where-
ever she passed, large marks of fresh blood.
Neither did her sufferings terminate with the
close of this martyrdom: for the wounds in her
tender flesh being irritated by a repetition of
such ill treatment, she continued for many days,
to feel the most acute pain.

Nor with all this was she yet satiated: on the
contrary the ardent desire, which she had of
suffering for her spouse, sharpened her wit to
discover new methods of tormenting herself.
And she invented one among the others as dangerous in its execution as it was painful to her,
and therefore more in accordance with her taste.
On Holy-Thursday she had scattered at the foot
of the altars of the *via crucis* various little bundles of sharp thorns, which she had provided
for this purpose. After this commencing according to custom to make the stations, when
she arrived at each one of them, she deposited
upon the ground and in the midst of the thorns
her cross, and after saying some prayers, begged
her companions, that when she would bend
down to kiss the sacred wood, they would give

4

her a violent push upon the head. And the request was made by her with such affection and
in so courteous a manner, that the little girls
without further consideration acquiesced by
pushing her head violently upon the thorns.
The stations being gone through together with
their reiterated sufferings that accompanied
them, the Blessed child got up with her face
horribly pierced and covered with blood, but
full of fervour and inexpressible joy. God so
disposed that neither her sister nor her brother-
in-law were ever aware of this cruel infliction,
to which they would without doubt have put a
stop; as also that none of the thorns should
ever once strike Mary Ann's eyes, which might
easily have happened.

Whatever work of penance she saw practiced by others, she made use of every means
not only to imitate it in herself, but to surpass
it, by adding other austerities to it of her own
invention. One year whilst assisting at Holy
Week, she was wonderfully taken with the discipline, and the adoration of the cross, which
she saw some devout christians practising.
Wherefore when she had returned home, she
immediately set about making several disci-

plines, which she afterwards distributed to her little friends, animating them by her example and inflamed words to scourge themselves for the love of Jesus, who had endured and suffered so much for their salvation. But as for the adoration of the cross, she wished that horrible torment, which we have described above, to be reserved entirely for herself. She encircled the cross which was to be adored and which was extended upon the ground, with many and sharp thorns: and when she bent down with her hands behind her upon her shoulders, in order to kiss it, her companions had, one at a time, to give her a good thrust: so that falling heavily upon the thorns, she rose with her face all pricked and pierced in a dreadful manner. But this time her relatives perceived the wounds, and discovering from the innocent children the cause, they forbad Mary Ann that dangerous and indiscreet penance: and she who would rather have died than commit the slightest act of disobedience against the command of her superiors instantly obeyed.

In order to disturb the little sleep, which she took at night, she devised a species of penance, which only her great desire of suffering could

have suggested to her mind. She provided herself with five stones of moderate size, and having excavated in the pavement at the foot of
her little altar, a cross, she placed in its cavity
these stones, but so arranged, that the unequal
parts of the stones might project above the sur-
face of the pavement. Here and there around
the cross she strewed a quantity of nettles and
other pungent herbs. Her bed being prepared
in this manner, every Friday night, after having first entreated her associates that they
would recommend her to her divine spouse, she
lay down to sleep, extending her arms upon the
cross, with a piece of wood for a pillow under
her head. The blessed little child continued,
as long as she could, motionless upon this horrible bed of torture: but if sometimes, either
overcome by sleep or pain, she allowed her body
to roll off the stones, on whatever side she
turned, falling with the whole weight of her
body upon these thorny herbs, she revenged
herself, as she was wont to say for insufferable
delicacy. Her companions who were alone
privy to this painful martyrdom, testified in the
process, that it was generally necessary for
them in the morning to lift her from off her bed;

but in proportion as she was exhausted in body
the vigour of her mind increased.

She would have done much more to satisfy
her insatiable love of penance, if she had not
been constrained to be continually with her
nieces, and have them witnesses of her actions.
Nevertheless she laboured with so much art and
industry, that in the end she succeeded in using
these very children as instruments to torment
her body, and not to be conscious of it. As if
a vain spirit of bravado actuated her, she began to say, that she, although she was the
youngest of them, had such force of mind as to
be able to sustain without flinching the onset of
the whole of them : and then challenge them to
come to the proof and try, if they could by
striking her draw from her lips a sign or any
expression of pain. The little children being
provoked in this manner, as was but natural,
made a simultaneous charge on the back of Mary
Ann and with all the force of their arms struck
her on all sides without measure or discretion.
And because she made as it were fun of their
weakness in order to excite them rather than
show any feeling, they became more than ever
vexed at their inability to elicit a word of com-

plaint, picked up the five stones, which she kept
as we said, in the cavity of the cross, and with
them unmercifully pounded her all over her body. This which was diversion for the girls,
but a terrible torture to Mary Ann lasted many
weeks and she would wished to have it repeated
every Monday and Wednesday : but at last her
companions, although simple and innocent, discovered by the livid spots and wounds the out-
rage they had committed on their holy mistress,
and refused to lend a helping hand to a work
that could not but be extremely painful to her.

It was when she was shut up in her room at
night, that she gave full scope to her fervour.
At that time not being observed by any one,
she cruelly scourged herself two or three different times, either with whips, or nettles and
other sharp-pointed thistles, which she secretly
collected in the domestic garden. An Indian
servant found her by accident thus engaged, and
being greatly surprised to see a little girl of not
more than six years of age, with a bundle of
nettles in her hand, striking herself upon her
naked shoulders, from which blood was pro-
fusely flowing, asked her in all simplicity, if
that cruel flagellation did not cause her pain ?

Yes, replied Mary Ann, I sensibly feel the weight of these blows: but I do so to satisfy for my sins. And I beg you for the love of God not to say a word about it to my relatives, but keep it secret.

———▸◂———

CHAPTER III.

THE SOLITARY AND PENITENTIAL LIFE WHICH SHE LED IN THE VILLA AND IN THE CITY; ATTEMPTS TWICE TO FLY FROM HOME TO GO AND CONVERT THE INFIDELS, AND TO LIVE IN SOLITUDE, AND IS PREVENTED BY ALMIGHTY GOD IN WONDERFUL WAYS.

BUT although the Blessed Mary Ann neglected no means to conceal those great and extraordinary acts of austerity and mortification which we have just related, still the paleness of her face, the extenuation of her body, and the almost total prostration of her strength were effects too plain and evident, and calculated of themselves to lead every one to the knowledge

of the cause.   Wherefore D. Girolama becoming
alarmed about the health of her little sister determined to remove her for a short time from
the daily solitude of the house and bring her
with the family to one of her villas about five
leagues distant, where she hoped, that the
change of scenery and the pleasures of the country would induce her to relax a little her way
of life.   As soon therefore as the weather permitted, they quitted Quito and came to Saguance,
which was the name of the villa.

But wherever she went, Mary Ann always
carried along that ardent spirit of fervour by
which God interiourly governed her.   As soon
as she was arrived at the villa, whilst the domestics were all busy in putting the house in
order, and her three nieces amusing themselves
by running about every where, as children are
wont to do, Mary Ann seeing the time favourable left the house and under pretence of diver-
ting herself for a little while in the open air,
unobserved by any one, entered and hid herself
in a neighbouring forest.   D. Girolama very
soon perceived the absence of her sister, and
being in some fear, gave immediate orders to
the servants and her maids to go every where

in search of her. And it pleased God that one
of the domestics should penetrate into the
thicket, and in his search amongst the thick
branches of the trees, discover the little child
at a distance. She was kneeling at the foot of
an old and withered trunk, which she had pic-
tured to herself as the column, at which her
spouse Jesus had been bound, and scourging
herself upon her naked shoulders with a hand-
ful of thorny thistles. The flesh was already
cut and bruised and the blood was falling in
drops upon the ground. The good servant astonished and horrified at what he saw, stood for
some time motionless, looking at the affecting
spectacle : then, without breathing, turned
round and ran to inform D. Girolama, who hurried to the spot with her daughters. It can
scarcely be believed how displeased the servant
of God was at being surprised in this act. She
blushed deeply, and covering herself immediately stood up, and as if nothing at all was the
matter, with a joyful face and beaming with
love joined her nieces and returned to the
house.

But she could never afterwards forget this
solitude. We must say, that God communica-

ted himself to her in an intimate manner, infusing into her mind the sweetest heavenly consolations. Wherefore, by divine disposition not having been prohibited by her sister, every time the blessed child would secretly withdraw from the house, she quickly flew to her favorite forest: and there she remained long hours pouring forth her heart in fervent colloquies with her Beloved. She rejoiced exceedingly that she was here observed by no one and could to her heart's content satisfy her ardent love of mortification. Three several times she was surprised, whilst scourging herself to blood. Nay more, the domestics whenever they missed her from the house always went to the woods, where they were certain of finding her.

Once she returned about dusk to her beloved retreat, but with her strength so completely exhausted, that being overcome by weariness and drowsiness she gently fell asleep in the arms of her sister D. Girolama. This sister, who tenderly loved her, held her quietly upon her bosom, and wishing to put her to bed to repose with greater comfort, began very carefully to undress her: and taking off her upper garments saw that her under dress was all bathed

in blood. D. Girolama was frightened at the
sight, and cautiously investigating the cause,
found that her little sister had her sides all
torn by a plant that was very thorny, which
was still bound tightly around her. The good
lady could not contain herself at the sight and
melting into tears raised her eyes and hands to
heaven, humbling herself before God, who
placed under her eyes an example of such austerity in that little innocent soul. Then moved
to pity for Mary Ann, she tried to free her body
from that unusual instrument of torture. But
notwithstanding all the care she took to perform it in the most delicate manner possible,
the little child perceived her, and between sleep
and awake, with an unconscious motion immediately placed her hands upon the thorny bandage and exclaimed—" Ah they are taking from
me my dearest delight." A little after, becoming perfectly conscious, when she first discovered herself in the arms of her sister her face
reddened with blushes, and without uttering a
word she quietly withdrew, leaving the other, I
know not, whether more surprised or grieved.

Such were the amusements and the childish
pastimes, which she enjoyed at the villa. Cer-

tain it is, that being about to return in a short
time to the city, nothing grieved her more than
the thought of abandoning her favorite retreat
in the woods, where God had imparted to her a
taste of the delights of Paradise, by closely
uniting her to himself by love. Notwithstanding this, she knew how to find her solitude
within the domestic walls. For the purpose of
distracting her a little from that continual application of mind, D. Girolama had ordered her
every day, at an appointed hour, to conduct her
three nieces, her sister D. Agnese de Paredes,
and D. Scolastica Sarmiento, who were all
brought up together, into the garden attached
to the house and try and procure them some innocent diversion. Mary Ann promptly obeyed :
and at the appointed hour never failed to call her
companions and with the greatest pleasure lead
them with her into the garden. Arrived there,
after she had engaged them in some of their
merry efforts, she would gradually withdraw,
and go in search of some remote and hidden
corner, where, taking occasion from the variety
of plants and flowers, and singing of little
birds, she raised her soul to the contemplation
of heavenly things, and to the love of her di-

vine spouse. She was seen walking along as
one wrapt in ecstacy, with her face inflamed,
her eyes swimming in tears and wholly absorpt
in God. At other times unable to master the
interior fire which was consuming her, she was
heard to give vent to it in inflamed sighs and
in short but ardent aspirations of affection. D.
Scolastica Sarmiento, and D. Maria di Casso,
eye-witnesses deposed in the juridical process,
that sometimes in order to temper this interior
heat, she would open her dress, and try to cool
her breast by exposing it to the open air, and
at other times taking a bundle of nettles in her
hand and striking herself with them, exclaim
in tender accents: Ah the right side of my loving spouse! Ah the pierced side of my crucified
Jesus! In consequence of the stings which
these nettles left, her breast was swollen and
'disfigured: and she immersed in an ocean of
sweetness, as it were out of her senses, did not
perceive that she was attentively observed by
her companions.

In proportion as her love towards God went
on increasing, her desire that all men should
know and love him also increased. Not satisfied with using all the means in her power to

direct in the right path her sisters, nieces, and
friends, with whom she conversed, she began to
aspire after more magnanimous undertakings.
Being often brought to the church of the Society
of Jesus, she had frequently heard them speak
in the sermons of the Missions of Japan, of
the Morea, of China, and of other parts of the
East Indies. Every day she received information at Quito of the vast provinces of Maragnone, *los Magnas*, where a countless number of
infidels were eternally lost without resource, the
few missionaries of the Society who laboured
there indefatigably, not being sufficient to supply
the wants. It seemed therefore to Mary Ann that
it would be her fault if so many people remained in the darkness of heathenism, nor did
she believe that the weakness of her sex and
the tender age of only seven or eight years
would be a sufficient excuse to justify her before God. It happened also, that at this time
they were celebrating in the church of the Society the solemn festival of the three holy Jesuits and Japanese Martyrs, Paul Miki, John de
Goto, and James Kisai, lately raised to the honours of the altar. Mary Ann, when she heard
in the panegerics the great sufferings which

they endured for the propogation and defence
of the holy faith, felt her zeal rekindled, and
the most lively desire took possession of her
heart to give in imitation of them her blood and
life for the love of Christ. Not being able any
longer to master these interior emotions, she determined to put them into immediate execution.
Wherefore calling aside her three nieces D. Giovanna, D. Sebastiana di Casso and D. Scolastica,
she disclosed to them in secret her intentions.
She told them that her heart was lively pierced
with grief at the sight of so many souls, who
in the country of the infidels, were travelling
the way of death, from the want of persons to
point out to them the road to heaven. That
she felt herself inspired to overcome all human
respect and go to the provinces of Maragnone,
where she hoped to rescue, with God's help, some
infidel from perdition and bring him to the
knowledge of the true God. That she would
consider herself happy, if in reward for her fa-
tigues, she could obtain the palm of martyrdom,
which others were fortunate enough to obtain.
That she thanked them for the good company
they had afforded her down to that time, and en-

treated them not to confide her resolution to any one before she had put it in execution.

The little girls were thrown into the utmost consternation when they heard the unexpected resolution she had formed, and grieving over the loss of their holy mistress, with tears in their eyes entreated her not to abandon them. That if nevertheless she was determined to go to the land of the infidels, not to disdain to have them also there as her companions, that they offered themselves with their whole heart to her: and after her example they promised to fear no dangers, not even death itself. Mary Ann delighted with having gained her companions over to her holy enterprise, accepted the offering, and fixed their flight for the following night. Their whole preparation consisted in providing a few clothes and a small quantity of biscuit; this alone seemed to them to be sufficient for a journey, of which they could form no conception. Nothing now remained but to secure the keys to open the door of the house: and this the blessed child undertook to manage. Finally the better to conceal their project, they all went early to bed. having agreed beforehand with Mary Ann. who was to wake them at a certain hour. Things

being brougnt to this point, God, who only desired the good will for the deed, by omens beyond the control of the children, willed that Mary
Ann should be overpowered by such a profound
sleep at the very time when she was always accustomed, about the middle of the night, to be
awake and to go to prayer, that she did not
open her eyes till it was broad day-light. Meanwhile the domestics were in search of the keys
of the house, and finding them near the servant
of God, gave notice of it to D. Cosimo and D.
Girolama, who easily understood the matter.
For the children frightened at seeing such a
commotion through the house, and believing for
certain that they were discovered, went immediately, as little innocent children always do, to
reveal to their parents, the secret of the pre-
meditated flight of their aunt to go and preach
the faith to the people of Maragnone.

Her first design having failed, and still feeling herself more than ever interiourly convinced that it was her duty to spend her life in
solitude, Mary Ann fixed on another plan which
seemed more easy to be carried out. There
was not very far from Quito a very high mountain called by the natives Picincia, on the top

of which was a terrible and frightful volcano.
The citizens in order to save their lives, because it often vomited forth quantities of ashes
and red-hot stones, had had recourse to the intercession of the most Blessed Virgin, and dedicated to her a little chapel on the side of the
mountain. In times past the veneration of the
people for this holy place was very great : but
their fervour afterwards cooling, it became almost entirely abandoned and neglected. It
seemed therefore to Mary Ann very well adapted to satisfy at the same time, her devótion
towards the Blessed Virgin and her desire of
living in solitude, by devoting herself to pass
her life in this retreat. She communicated her
new project to her companions ; and they immediately approving of it, offered themselves anew
to follow her. Before, however, putting their
plan in execution, they assembled many days together to discuss and establish the form and
tenour of their solitary life. And first of all
that none of the citizens, coming up the mountain of Picincia, might be ever able to know
them, they resolved to wound their faces with
pieces of glass and then fill the incisions with
coal dust, and thus disfigure themselves in such

a manner as to defy all recognition. They had
seen this done by the Indians of the savage
tribes, who frequently came down to Quito to
make a display of their horrid beauty. As for
their dress it was determined, that it should be
coarse and out of fashion, contenting themselves
to wear patched clothes as became those who
wished to lead a poor and penitential life in an
hermitage: and for food they agreed, that
every week upon a certain day one of them
should descend from the mountain and go and
beg from door to door in the city a little bread
for the *poor slaves of Mary*, by which name
they were to be called.

These things being resolved upon by common
consent, they only waited a favourable opportunity of secretly leaving the house : which was
to be done, not by night as was formerly intended, but in broad day-light, in order to give
less ground for suspicion to their parents. Nor
had they to wait long; for having discovered
that D. Cosimo and D. Girolama had gone to
the country at no great distance from the city
about some business and would remain there
several days, they began to prepare without delay for their departure; and taking a bundle

containing some clothes and a small provision
of food, secretly left the house, and took a by-
path that led towards the mountain. And they
had already ascended half-a-league up the ac-
clivity, and being well satisfied with the good
success of their flight, were praising and
thanking God, when a wild bull darting
suddenly from the neighbouring forest made
strait at them with bended head to gore them.
To escape from the danger that threatened
them, they found no better way than to throw
themselves in haste into a ditch, that was aside
of the road and there protected, wait till the
beast would either turn back or proceed on.
And when they saw that he had gone away to
some distance from them, coming forth from
their place of security, they courageously started
to resume their march. But behold the bull
returns to the charge with more ferocity than
ever: and so, as often as they attempted to go
forward on their way, so often did the animal
return to stop them. Mary Ann was much
more grieved at this than any of her companions; and fully persuaded that it was the devil,
who taking that form endeavored to turn them
from their holy resolution, tried frequently

with the sign of the cross, to put him to flight:
but seeing that this did no good, she drew
aside and kneeling down turned to consult God
to know what she should do. The short prayer
ended, the Lord, who this time only required of
her a promptness of will, made her distinctly
hear in her soul an interior voice, which told
her, that it was the will of heaven, that she
should lead a life perfectly estranged from the
things of the world, not in a desert place, but
indeed in her own house: wherefore having joined
her companions, " God, " said she, " does not
wish us to go to the desert; but wishes that we
turn back; and we must obey him." These
words were hardly uttered by Mary Ann, before the bull ceased to threaten them, and dis-
appearing in the woods they soon lost sight of
him. Then the little girls, turned their backs
to the mountain, and believing that their flight
was not yet discovered by the domestics, hastened to re-enter the house. But they were
disappointed in their hopes: for the servants
being informed of the departure of the little
girls and aware of the flight once before attempted, immediately suspected the true cause,
and informed D. Girolama of it, who was then

returned to the city, and who easily obtained a full account from her daughters of the whole adventure.

————•←————

CHAPTER IV.

SHE IS NOT YET EIGHT YEARS OF AGE AND IS ADMIT-
TED TO HOLY COMMUNION, FOR WHICH SHE PRE-
PARES HERSELF WITH GREAT FERVOUR AND DE-
RIVES ABUNDANT FRUIT FROM IT. SHE CONSE-
CRATES HERSELF TO GOD BY THE THREE SIMPLE
VOWS OF POVERTY, CHARITY AND OBEDIENCE.
GIVES HERSELF UP ENTIRELY TO THE DIRECTION
OF HER CONFESSOR, AND SUFFERS CONTRADIC-
TIONS AND OPPOSITION ON ACCOUNT OF HER
DAILY COMMUNION.

THESE were, as every one sees, interiour impul-
ses of grace, which was disposing the Blessed
Mary Ann for that austere and penitential life,
which she afterwards led for the space of fourteen years. But not knowing yet distinctly what

was the divine will in this, nor having those who
would be its interpreters, as she had not yet given
herself up to the guidance of her confessors, it frequently happened that she lent a willing ear to
every good emotion that sprung up in her heart
and endeavored to second it as much as she
could, following rather the impetus of her fervour than the proper rules of discretion. Hence
it was, that whilst God on the one side pleased
with her readiness, accepted the good will, in
wonderful ways on the other side prevented the
execution of it.

As for the rest, in proportion as the servant
of God advanced in years, her soul daily increased in perfection. A disrelish and disgust
for the things of the earth, a love of solitude
and silence, a fervour of piety and devotion, an
intimate communication and familiarity with God,
and a continual penitential vigour, notwithstanding the extreme purity, and the greatest
delicacy of conscience were every day more and
more visible in her. All these things well considered induced D. Girolama to think that she
ought no longer to deprive that innocent soul
of the participation of the holy mysteries, and
particularly of holy communion, for which she

seemed so well disposed. The only difficulty in
the way was her tender age, as she had not yet
completed her eighth year. But there was no
cause for delaying on this account: because
Mary Ann had not only acquired the perfect
use of reason, which in her certainly anticipated her years, but in all her actions displayed
such maturity of sense and ripeness of judgment, that she astonished all who conversed
with her. It only then remained to see, if she
were well instructed in the mysteries of faith,
and if she sufficiently comprehended the things
which are proposed to our belief in the most
adorable sacrament of the Eucharist. To clear
up this point she was examined by wise and
prudent men, who were struck at the depth of
knowledge she displayed in her first answers to
their questions, and as is recorded in the process, were of opinion, that such knowledge in
her was not natural, but supernaturally infused
by God. Because, they found that she not only
believed with the strongest conviction, but spoke
in terms of the most abstruse and hidden mysteries, as if she had them before her corporal
eyes; and as for her interior disposition, she
had languished for a long time with the mos

ardent desire, and eagerly panted to be fed on
the bread of angels. D. Girolama being informed of all this, immediately told her sister
to get ready to make her first communion at the
approaching festival.

At this good news, the virgin of Christ ex-
ulted with joy, and began forthwith to prepare
the habitation for her beloved spouse. She redoubled her fasts, which were already three
days a week, on bread and water: increased the
measure of her other penances and the fervour
of her prayers. When the appointed day arrived, she was conducted by her sister to the
church of the Society of Jesus, and consigned
to Father John Camaccio to hear her confession.
This Religious was a man of much virtue and
learning, besides being very expert in conducting souls to the highest perfection. He was
teaching at the time Theology, and as General
Prefect of studies, presided over our University
of St. Gregory. After hearing her general confession, which the Servant of God wished to
make from the first moments of her recollection, he remained as it were beside himself with
wonder, in seeing in a little girl of a few years,
knowledge so profound and such lofty senti-

ments of God and heavenly things, and above
all the most ardent desires of aspiring by the
practice of virtue, to the most sublime and heroic sanctity. After this he not only comforted
her by permitting her to approach the eucharistic table, but gently remonstrated with her
sister D. Girolama, for having so long deprived
that innocent and pure soul, free from every
earthly blemish, of the salutary grace of the
sacraments. Mary Ann also in her turn was
enraptured with the wisdom and goodness of
her confessor, and resolved forthwith to give
herself up entirely to his guidance and direction in her spiritual concerns.

I will not attempt to describe the interiour
affection, with which she received her Lord in
the sacrament of the altar, nor the interiour delights, which she enjoyed that day. Being hidden things, we can form no correct judgment of
them. We can, however, from that little, which
was exteriourly manifested in her actions, make
some conjecture of how much was concealed
within her soul. When therefore she had
poured forth her soul for a considerable time in
returning thanks to Almighty God, she returned
home and full of an unusual joy which shone

upon her face, called her nieces, and said to
them: That henceforth they were to respect her
tongue and venerate her soul, which had been
sanctified that morning by coming in contact
with her immaculate Spouse Jesus. After this
she divested herself of a beautiful little
silk dress, which D. Girolama had wished her
to use for the occasion; and with ardent prayers
entreated her never more to think of providing
her with ornaments of that description, which
she could not bear to wear. The only bitterness and confusion she experienced on that day,
she said, was that very silk dress, which was
not for her; and consequently that every hour
seemed a thousand years before she could
return home and lay aside that miserable vanity.
And she added with much feeling, that being
born, not to please the eyes of men, but solely
to become acceptable to her heavenly Spouse,
she had no need of adoring her body with out-
ward garments, but to deck her soul every day
more and more with the garb of virtue. And
that she said the truth she quickly proved by
facts, generously retrenching every thing, that
savoured of earth and the world, and devoting
herself a perfect holocaust to the service and

love of God. She renounced the title of *Donna*, which, according to the custom of the country belonged to her by right of birth and nobility of family ; and that all might know, that she was no longer, to use the expression, her own property, but belonged entirely to her heavenly Spouse, she assumed the name of *Mary Ann of Jesus*, nor from that time did she wish to be otherwise addressed ; and finally she bound herself by vow to preserve her purity unspotted till her death.

This was the rich fruit, which the Blessed Mary Ann derived from her first communion. And I would wish that certain parents, who delay so long to make their children partake of the holy sacraments, would learn a useful lesson from the example before them. They wait till the devil and sin enter to darken and destroy the purity and innocence of their souls, whilst Jesus Christ and his grace ought to be the first to take possesion of them and render them strong and generous by their presence against the assaults of their enemies. Boys and girls may also learn hence, with what dispositions they ought to come prepared to receive the eucharistic bread, and with what diligence guard and increase the fruit they receive. As for Mary Ann, she derived such strength from the first taste of those heavenly delights, with which she felt her whole soul inundated by her divine guest, that she did not know how to fix bounds to her progress in holiness. All her thoughts and affections were for Jesus : and for many days afterwards she could speak but of him, nor desire aught but him. The fulness of the grace received, instead of satiating her, had excited in her the greatest hunger for this divine bread : and therefore not being able to resist its cravings, she went immediately to Father Camaccio her confessor, and humbly entreated him to give her permission frequently to approach the eucharistic table.

But the Father, who had discovered in her from the time of her first confession a soul capable of every degree of advancement in perfection, did not wish immediately to satisfy all her desires, but pretended to oppose and contradict her wishes. And when he saw that the Servant of God promptly obeyed and submitted to every proof, he applied himself with much -care to cultivate her soul. And first of all he acquainted her with the spiritual exercises of

St. Ignatius; and in them he explained to her
the practical method of praying mentally, of
contemplating with fruit the divine mysteries
of the life and passion of Jesus Christ: of pu-
rifying the conscience every day by means of
the two examens, general and particular: of
correcting, discerning and judging the spirits,
which move us to act, and of knowing which
are good and safe, which bad and deceitful; all
according to the wise prescriptions and rules
given by the Saint in his admirable book of
the spiritual exercises. Of the penances some
were allowed, others denied her: and finally as
for communion it was determined, that for the
present she might receive every Sunday, and
every festival that happened to come during the
week.

Thus she increased every day, more and more
in virtue, when, on reaching her tenth year, she
felt herself inspired to consecrate herself wholly to God and unite herself to him by closer
ties, renouncing all the things of the earth and
divesting herself of her own will. Wherefore
when she renewed her vow of perpetual
chastity made two years before, she added

the two other simple vows of poverty and
obedience. Father Camaccio was not pleased
that she had presumed, without consulting him,
to bind herself by ties so indissoluble. Therefore to put her virtue to the test, he refused to
ratify what she had done; and in the meanwhile, carefully observed the new way of life,
which she would lead. But after a short time,
seeing the great strides which she made towards
the summit of perfection, he not only approved
of the vows she had made, but permitted her to
renew them, as she did, writing also two copies
of the formula, one of which she retained, and
the other she gave to her confessor. Of all the
property that her parents left her for a dowry,
she kept nothing for herself, but made a dona-
tion of the whole of it to D. Giovanna her
niece; and as for habitation and food, she threw
herself upon the charity of her sister D. Girolama. We shall see in its proper place, how
perfectly she observed these three vows. Let
it suffice for the present to say, that according
to the depositions of her confessors, she was
never guilty in the whole course of her life, of
a breach of them that would amount to a full,
deliberate venial sin. And she was not a Reli-

gious confined to a cloister, but a secular in the
world, in the midst of the difficulties and dangers
of an universal corruption.

It is true, that she drew her whole strength
from the union with her heavenly Spouse in the
holy communion.   Wherefore, not content with
receiving him every Sunday and festival of the
year, she earnestly entreated her confessor, to
allow her to approach oftener: and he becoming
more liberal, permitted her to receive holy communion three times a week.   This however
only served to increase the hunger of her pure
soul which was enamoured with God.   She was
interiourly inflamed with the most ardent desire
of receiving still oftener Jesus Christ within her
bosom; and awaited with the greatest anxiety the day, on which, according to the permission of her confessor, she could approach the
holy table.   It was observed, that that wonderful prodigy was renewed in her, which the holy
Scriptures relate of the prophet Elias, who
being fed with that food that was miraculously
brought him, walked with strength and vigour
unto the holy mount of God.   Mary Ann after
communicating, felt such vigour and strength
of spirit, which overflowing, and as it were,

taking possession of her, she needed during
that day, no material food to support her. On
the contrary, on the day that intervened, and on
which she had to abstain from the food of the
strong, she seemed sensibly to languish as it
were, for want of food, and from loss of
strength, to need frequent sustenance. Father
Camaccio, to whom the servant of God every
day rendered an exact account of her conscience,
knew her sufferings; and at last considering
the extreme purity of her soul, and the ardent
love she has for Jesus, after recommending the
matter to God with many prayers, determined
to allow her to approach daily. But he first
asked her, what was the preparation she was
accustomed to make, and being told, that her
care was always to strive, that her union with
her heavenly Spouse should every day increase,
and become more intimate: and therefore studied to seek him and love him more and more.
Hearing this, it did not seem to him that he
ought to deprive Mary Ann any longer of that
great happiness; and gave her permission to approach every day.

Whilst the servant of God was, as it were,
out of herself with the joy she had received,

there suddenly rose one of the most furious
storms of contradictions against her. In those
days the faithful were not much in the habit of
frequenting the holy table ; and those who approached every eighth day were considered far
advanced in the things of God. As soon as it
was known therefore, that Mary Ann, a little
girl who at the time had hardly passed her
twelfth year, communicated every day with the
approbation of her director, some began to murmur, and in a short time, as is always the case,
she was the common talk all over the city.
Every one wished to meddle in the matter and
to censure her without mercy : and not alone
the common people, but men also very much esteemed for learning and piety, who from not
knowing Mary Ann, judged her according to
the common report which was circulated about.
They did not deny that she was a child of irre-
proachable morals and of an angelical purity;
nevertheless that she was too young and perhaps, for want of sufficient reason, not even arrived at a proper age to understand the mysteries, that are contained in that most august sacrament. That daily communion was with difficulty allowed to persons of a mature age, of

solid virtue, enclosed in a monastery, or distinguished by Almighty God with particular marks
of favour. What discretion was there then in
granting it to a little child of twelve years of
age, living in the midst of the world and its
distractions? Father Camaccio had enough to
do to defend himself and his penitent : because
the rumour instead of dying away increased
daily : and reached such a point that it excited
the fears and suspicion of the Superiours of the
Society and of the Episcopal officers of Quito.
Mary Ann was very much afflicted, not so much
for herself, as for her director, upon whom the
heaviest censures fell, as a man of little wisdom
and experience in guiding souls in the way of
virtue. Nevertheless she was never for a moment discouraged or dejected in the midst of so
much contradiction; but whilst on the one side
she suffered every thing with perfect resignation
to the divine will and endured it with patience,
her great love for Jesus Christ in the sacrament,
on the other, rendered her courageous to sur-
mount every obstacle. And speaking one day
with her confessor, who seeing the brand of
discord ignited, was at a perfect loss to know
what to do, she encouraged him to place his

trust in God who would put a term to this opposition; "my father," said she, "let us confide
inthe Lord; that his holy will be done, and not
that of men." And it turned out just as she had
predicted. For the Bishop, in order to do away
with every cause of contention and disagree-
ment, called before him a council of the
wisest and most learned men, and in the presence also of the Superiours of the Religious
Orders wished that the *pro & con* of the cause
should be examined: and as Almighty God
wished, urged by the weight of the reasons
brought forward, with one common accord, they
approved the conduct of Father Camaccio, and
left the servant of God full liberty to communicate every day. It is true that some individuals
did not cease therefore to scoff at her for some
time: but she was not at all disturbed, and
only in order to prevent their talk, she prudently
strove to communicate at a mass, which was
said very late, and at a time when few persons
were in the church. The fame of her admirable sanctity being afterwards increased, not
only the tongues of her enemies were silenced,
but they were all turned into the highest com-
mendation of her. A few years later, Father
Camaccio having been obliged to quit Quito, she

chose successively for her directors the very
fathers, who had shown themselves somewhat
opposed to her on this point; and all of them
as soon as they saw by what spirit she was guided, condemned themselves as rash in having
prejudged without a knowledge of the cause.
Thus ended this no small contraction raised
against the servant of God.

CHAPTER V.

SEVERAL TIMES THE BLESSED MARY ANN IS ON THE
    VERY POINT OF ENTERING A MONASTERY TO BE-
    COME A RELIGIOUS, BUT IS ALWAYS PREVENTED
    BY ALMIGHTY GOD FROM EXECUTING HER RESO-
    LUTION, FINALLY BY A SPECIAL LIGHT FROM
    HEAVEN SHE DETERMINES TO LEAD A SOLITARY
    LIFE IN HER OWN HOUSE.   SHE DETACHES HER-
    SELF FROM EVERY EARTHLY THING, AND TAKES
    LEAVE OF HER RELATIONS.   HER PROPHECIES :
    AND A REMARKABLE OCCURRENCE THAT HAP-
    PENED TO HER NIECE D. SEBASTIANA.

THE great retirement in which the Blessed
Mary Ann lived, devoting herself entirely to

7

the exercise of the most heroic virtues, and
above all the knowledge that she was already
consecrated to God by the three vows of poverty, chastity and obedience, which constitute
the religious state, induced D. Cosimo her brother-in-law and D. Girolama her sister to think she
would be much pleased if they proposed to her
to become an inmate of some monastery of virgins for the purpose of finishing her education,
and afterwards should it be the will of Almighty
God. make her religious profession.   The servant of God was not at all opposed to it: on
the contrary having contracted a friendship with
the Mother Anna di S. Paolo, superioress of
the monastery of St. Catherine, she one day
asked her with much humility to be admitted
for the present as a scholar, until she would
discover by a heavenly light whether she was to
consecrate herself irrevocably therein or not.
This was the very thing these good Religious
ladies desired, who had long known the extraordinary virtues of Mary Ann; and therefore
having resolved that she should enter the monastery that very day, and as nothing was wanting but the consent of her brother-in-law D.
Cosimo, they sent immediately in search of him

to the public square, where generally he was
accustomed to amuse himself at that hour with
other gentlemen.   But in spite of all their mes-
sengers and the inquiries they made, he was not
to be found: and the consequence was that not
being able to conclude the affair, Mary Ann
towards dusk returned home; and having afterwards related to D. Cosimo all that had taken place
during the day, he was very much surprised, saying that he had never left the public square, nor
could he understand why he had not been seen
by some one of the many passengers, who went
in search of him: and concluded, that it was
perhaps a particular dispensation of the Almighty,
who did not approve of the resolution she had
taken.

After some months, D. Cosimo was the first
to propose to his sister-in-law to become a Religious; and because some impediments had
arisen to prevent her entrance among the Religious of St. Catherine, he suggested to her to
become a nun in the convent of St. Clare. And
Mary Ann having told him, that she would willingly enter that monastery, if such were the
will of God, D. Cosimo not reflecting on the
condition, but taking her answer as absolutely

affirmative, began immediately to prepare every thing requisite for her solemn entrance. The nuns were already informed of it, the relatives of the family and the nobility invited, the day fixed, and every thing arranged with much expense and pomp, as was befitting the rank and birth of the young lady. Mary Ann alone in the midst of all this preparation, contrary to her usual custom, remained cold and indifferent, as if the matter did not at all regard her. Recollecting that interiour voice she once heard on mount Picincia, by which it appeared to be the will of God, that she should lead a retired life in her own home, and no where else, she withdrew in silence to her room, and with many prayers and penances besought her divine Spouse to guide her in her deliberation and make known to her his divine will. She had not to wait long to receive the grace. We know not how; but it is certain, that she was so fully persuaded and convinced that she was not to lead a religious life in a monastery, but remain a secular in her own home, that not the smallest doubt or suspicion could exist of an illusion or deceit. Afterwards going to the church, Father Camaccio before hearing her confession, asked her

when she intended to enter the monastery. And
she replied immediately with much firmness,
that she could never enter. The Father won-
dered very much at this answer. "What do you
tell me, never!" said he: "is not every thing
prepared, and only a few days remaining before
you enter?" And still it is so, she again replied
in a firm voice: I will not enter, because my
Spouse does not wish it. Mary Ann was always very guarded in speaking, especially of
herself and her affairs: consequently her confessor hearing her reply with such assurance,
quickly judged, that she had had some special
inspiration from God, and ordered her on the
spot to declare what it was. The servant of
the Lord promptly obeyed, and opening her
whole soul to him, told him frankly, what by
the light of prayer, she had clearly discovered:
and he was not only satisfied, but so convinced
of the thing, that he took upon himself the task
of speaking to D. Cosimo and D. Girolama, representing to them, that it was the express will
of God, that Mary Ann should not shut herself
up in a monastery, but lead a life of retirement
in her own home.

It did not appear, to tell the truth, such an

easy matter to change in an instant the will and
judgment of D. Cosimo, who, although he was a
man of much virtue, was nevertheless naturally
very sensitive and jealous of his honour. It
was feared, therefore, that having already concluded the contract with the nuns, and pledged
his word with the nobility, he would not be so
easily induced to retrace his steps and undo
what was already done at the expense of his reputation. Notwithstanding all this, as God directed every thing, so, by the Divine disposal,
no difficulty or obstacle was met with on this
point. Father Camaccio, accompanied by Father
Anthony Monosalvas, who was afterwards also
the confessor of Mary Ann, went to visit him,
and in few words told him the occasion of their
visit. And that it might more clearly appear
that God directed the whole affair, the Father
had no sooner concluded his discourse, than, as
is recorded in the juridical process, D. Cosimo
and D. Girolama threw themselves on their
knees, and raising their hands to heaven, declared, " We neither wish nor desire aught than
that the will of the Lord be done and accomplished in all things." And immediately, with
great peace and tranquillity of mind, they gave

orders for the suspension of every thing, and
after offering as a present to Mary Ann all that
had been prepared for her entrance into the monastery, assigned her, for her place of retirement, a certain apartment of the house divided
into several rooms.

The Blessed Mary Ann rejoiced beyond measure to see the final accomplishment of her desires, distributed to the poor whatever had been
given her as a present by her relatives, and
sedulously set about preparing the suite of
apartments in which God called her to lead a
life truly extraordinary. And the first thing
she did was to remove all the rich and sump-
tuous furniture from the rooms, retaining only
a few chairs, a small table, and a miserable
little bed, which she never used, but which
served to hide her austerities from the eyes of
others. She selected these and a few other
pieces of furniture from among the meanest of
the house, but they were all decent and clean:
for, as she herself was all purity in soul and body
she abhorred every appearance of filth. Besides this, she supplied herself with every description of penitential instruments—hair-shirts,
chains, disciplines, crosses, and, moreover, a

coffin—for what use, we will see afterwards.
In the most private and secret corner she erected a little altar, that had more devotion about
it than riches, and on it she placed the little
statues of the Infant Jesus and the Blessed Virgin, which had been from her infancy the fond-
est objects of her love. Around the naked wall
she hung many crosses, and the simple images of
the saints, her patrons and advocates. Lastly,
she ordered a lock to be fixed on the inside of
her apartment, that could not be opened from
without; having from the beginning resolved
to admit no one, not even her nearest relatives,
into her rooms.

With respect to dress, she absolutely laid aside
every article that could be of ornament, and also
those made of linen. For her under-dress she
used a thick and common canvass, much used by
the common country people, but so artfully
made, that the few trimmings by which it was
encircled, and which appeared around the neck,
were of a somewhat better and finer texture,
and thus none could see the haircloth that was
next her person; her dress was a gown of black
serge, much like that of the Fathers of the Society, without a collar, and open above and be-

low, which was fastened to her body with a belt
from which hung the rosary of the Most Blessed
Virgin; her head was covered with a large veil,
likewise black, which, falling over her shoulders,
covered her whole person as far as the feet, like
a cloak.   I find it recorded in the process, that
she carried also on her breast the most holy
name of Jesus, by which she always wished to be
addressed, wrought in her dress.   Hence it was
that, as we find in the process, on account of her
peculiar form of dress, and her constant attend-
ance at the church of the Jesuits, she was com-
monly called *the Oblate of the Society :* but the
truth is, she had no other intimacy with the Society but a great love and affection for it, as she
had always been directed in spiritual matters
by the members of the Society, and on account
of her desire to conform, in as much as she
could, to the rules of the Order, especially in
those things which regarded her interiour.

Every thing being now arranged, and being
on the point of shutting herself up, a voluntary
recluse in her domestic solitude, Mary Ann
wished to bid an affectionate farewell, first to
her relatives, who were out of the house, then to
the family itself, as if she were never more to

see them in this world. But the parting scene between her and her three nieces, with whom she had been brought up, was by far the most touching. Sending for them, she conducted them to a retired spot, and there, with many expressions of affection, told them of the resolution she had formed, and the new kind of solitary life, which, by the Divine appointment, she was about to commence; that every thing was now ready, and that nothing remained but to shut herself up in her voluntary retreat, which the charity of their parents had prepared for her; that she had therefore wished to see them first, and to bid them a lasting farewell; to thank them for their agreeable conversation and company, which she had enjoyed up to that hour, in her daily intercourse with them; and if, in the frequent communication they had had together, she had been an occasion of scandal, or bad example, to ask pardon and forgiveness of them; that she had seen nothing but what was praiseworthy in their conduct, which had always been extremely edifying, or in their morals, which had been, by the protection of God, innocent and pure—they should recollect, however, that the enemies of their salvation would never

cease to lay their snares and devices to divert
them from the right path; that it was necessary to watch continually over themselves, and,
armed by a holy fear of God, to maintain themselves firm and constant in the exercise of the
virtues heretofore practised; they should take
to heart solid piety and devotion, nourishing
them by the frequentation of the holy sacraments, nor suffer themselves to be seduced by
the follies of the world and vain hopes, which so
many unfortunate youths place in the vigour of
youth, beauty of person, and in the abundance
of riches. Then, with her heart upon her lips,
remembering the tender love she had always
borne them, as to the companions from her
childhood of her devotions, she begged them
that they would never forget to recommend her
often to the Lord. For the rest, that when she
would be once shut up in her retirement, they
should look upon Mary Ann from that day as
dead; for such was the will of her Divine Spouse.

In saying this, and scarcely able to restrain her
tears, on account of the interiour commotion experienced, she extended her arms to embrace
them; but the children, surprised by the novelty of the thing, whilst Mary Ann was speak-

ing, had remained as it were astonished and out
of themselves; scarcely had she finished, when
they drew back, bursting into a flood of tears.
They were inconsolable at the announcement of
this bitter and unexpected separation; and therefore, after giving way for some little time to
their sighs and tears, they humbly entreated
their loving aunt to admit them all three into
her solitude; and when they were told that such
was not the will of God, seized with a new ardour, they offered to consecrate themselves,
after her exemple, spouses of Jesus Christ by a
perpetual vow of chastity. The saint was delighted to see so much fervour in her nieces;
and at the same moment, being enlightened from
above, and foreseeing what was to happen, told
D. Giovanna that God did not wish that vow
from her, having destined her for the state of
matrimony, and then she distinctly pointed out
to her the endowments and the qualities of the
individual who would be her husband. Afterwards turning to the other two, D. Maria and
D. Sebastiana, she exhorted them to be constant
in their resolution, which God had graciously
accepted; and to D. Sebastiana in particular,
she added, that her virtue would be put to a

severe trial; that she must not on that account
lose courage, and should it cost her her life, to
preserve the promise and faith pledged to her
Divine Spouse. And it came to pass just as
she had predicted. D. Giovanna led an edifying life in the marriage state; and we shall
speak of her several times in the course of this
history, when we recount the singular favours
she received from God through the intercession
of Mary Ann, still living. D. Maria consecrated
herself to God in a monastery of barefooted
Carmelites, where, ripe 'in age and merits, she
died in the odour of sanctity: she long survived
the servant of God, and could consequently depose in the process to the wonderful things which
she had seen with her own eyes, D. Sebastiana
was still more fortunate, who obtained of God
the happiness of dying rather than lose the
flower of her virginity; and she had the privilege of having her blessed aunt to assist her in
the last moments of her extraordinary death.
The fact, although recorded in the process,
escaped the notice of the first writer of Mary
Ann's life; and I, in order not to transfer the
recital of it to a more distant page, will give it
here, where it suits my purpose.

D. Sebastiana being in her thirteenth or
fourteenth year, and, moreover, desirous of following the example of her sainted aunt, with
many prayers entreated her to admit her into
her apartment, that they might there lead together a life entirely separated from the world,
and united to God. At first Mary Ann refused
to accede to her request; but afterwards, moved
by the perseverance of her niece, who every day
renewed her petition, finally consented, and
gave her a room at a little distance from her
own, in order that she might not discover the
wonderful austerity she practised. D Sebastiana, overjoyed to have obtained her object,
took up her abode in the apartment of her
aunt; and that she might never more be separated from her, by her counsel, and with the
approbation of her confessor, she bound herself
to God by a perpetual vow of chastity· Several
years had passed since they began to lead together this angelical life, when, one day, the
saint, in a conversation with her sister, D. Girolama, accidentally heard her say that Sebastiana had been betrothed to a young man as
distinguished for his nobility as he was for his
virtue. At which she was very much surprised,

and interrupted her, to tell her that she must take care what she did; that such certainly was not her daughter's intention, who had, several years previously, made a vow of chastity. D. Girolama, astonished also in her turn, was for some time lost in thought; after that, replied with much sorrow, that it was now too late; that not only had they pledged their word, and concluded the contract, but that the expenses had already been incurred, and every prepara- tion made for solemnizing the marriage. Having heard this, Mary Ann immediately retired to her chamber, and having called her niece to her, " Do you know," said she, " that your parents have already disposed of you to an earthly man? Now what will you do, having promised to Jesus Christ to preserve your virginity unspotted?" The young girl, at this unexpected news, was dissolved in tears; then suddenly recovering herself, " Very well," she replied, " I shall ask my Divine Spouse to take me to himself, by re- moving me out of this life before the day ap- pointed for the nuptials arrives." Mary Ann approved of her resolution, and exhorted her to implore this grace of God, as she was sure to obtain it: and both of them immediately knelt

down to pray. After their prayer was finished,
she sent her niece to bed, who was taken, that
very same night, with a very violent fever:
wherefore, early next morning, the Saint went
to her sister to tell her that Sebastiana was
dangerously ill; that she should think of trans-
ferring her into her own room, and afterwards
might give her a husband, if she wished. The
physicians were quickly summoned, and every
remedy was tried, but all to no purpose; for,
instead of getting better, she gradually grew
worse. In the meantime the servant of God
asked her sister to have some fresh bunches of
flowers brought; " because," said she, " we must
begin to prepare for the funeral obsequies of
Sebastiana." These words pierced D. Girolama
to the heart, who, turning to Marn Ann, said,
" You are determined, it seems, on the death of
my daughter." She had, nevertheless, the flowers
for which she had asked; and so entertained
herself for several hours in the room of the invalid, talking of the happiness of heaven, and
weaving together garlands, crowns, and festoons,
such as they are accustomed to strew on the
corpses of deceased virgins. When their work
was ended, the Saint stood up and spoke in

secret, for some time, to the invalid; after that,
with much hilarity, taking leave of her sister,
there present, "Good-by," said she, "I am going to leave Sebastiana in Paradise." To whom
D. Girolama, deeply oppressed with grief, replied, "Go, my sister; you have already sent
her there by express." Mary Ann left, to shut
herself up in her retreat; and the invalid within an hour, without any sign of pain or agony,
calmly expired. D. Girolama ran immediately,
with her hair dishevelled, and weeping bitterly,
to inform her sister; and having knocked several times at the door, and seeing she did not
answer, nor open it, by pushing, she broke the
bolt on the inside, and entering, found the servant of God on her knees, in an ecstacy, before
her little altar, with her eyes raised to heaven,
and perfectly motionless. She tried to recall
her to herself by shaking her by the clothes,
and calling her in a loud voice; but finding it
useless, she went away, leaving her still in an
ecstacy. A little after, Mary Ann came forth
from her room, and, with her face inflamed, and
every appearance of joy about her, meeting her
sister, D. Girolama, "Oh, let us thank the Lord,"
said she; "Sebastiana is already in company

8*

with her Divine Spouse : weep not, but rejoice
that you have acquired a son-in-law of such a
high and divine lineage : you have married your
daughter to Jesus Christ for all eternity. Happy
would we be, if we could now enjoy her lot !"
Having said this, she retired again to her apartment, very much agitated in mind by her interiour emotions of affection. She wished afterwards to be present at the public and solemn
obsequies which were performed for her niece
in the Church of St. Francis, whither a great
concourse of persons had assembled, drawn
thither by the report of this wonderful occurrence, which quickly circulated all over the city,
and the recollection of which continued for many
years afterwards.

CHAPTER VI.

THE RIGID COURSE OF LIFE WHICH THE BLESSED
MARY ANN COMMENCED TO LEAD IN HER RETIRE-
MENT. THE ORDER AND DISTRIBUTION OF HER
ACTIONS. THE INVENTIONS AND STRANGE CON-
TRIVANCES TO TORMENT HER BODY, AND THE
HORRIBLE MANNER IN WHICH SHE TREATED IT.
THE ARDENT DESIRE SHE HAD OF SHEDDING HER
BLOOD FOR THE LOVE OF JESUS CHRIST: IT IS
REWARDED BY ALMIGHTY GOD WITH WONDERFUL
PRODIGIES.

To return to our history. When the Blessed
Mary Ann of Jesus had bidden her last farewell
to her relatives, her nieces, to every thing which
belonged to the flesh and the world, she at length
shut herself up in her long-wished for retreat.
She was only in her twelfth year; and continued
for about fourteen years—that is to say, to her
death—to lead a solitary life, separated entirely
from the world, and devoted exclusively to the
contemplation of heavenly things, and the mortification of her innocent and virginal body.

I will proceed, taking each thing up successively, and place them distinctly before the
reader; and first, I will relate that uncommon
and extraordinary rigour which she practised in
every kind of austerity and penance. To diminish the wonder, and I would almost say, the
horror, which the sight of these corporal inflic-
tions might naturally excite in us, considering
that she who exercised them was one of unspotted innocence, and therefore had nothing to
atone for, we must again remind the reader of
what we said before, that God by many signs
had clearly manifested his wish to conduct his
servant by ways out of the usual course, and
therefore had given her spirit and strength to
support the enormous weight of the most terrible penances, which were far beyond the frailty
of human nature to endure. Father Camaccio,
her confessor, had often thought, from the first
time he undertook the direction of her soul, to
forbid her, under virtue of obedience, the practice of such cruel austerity towards herself; but
he confessed that he had always been prevented,
and that, guided by some secret inspiration, he
had suddenly changed his mind; so that he
could do no more than occasionally moderate

their rigour, especially in time of sickness.
Her relatives also, being afraid that they would
lose her in a short time, complained bitterly,
and exhorted her to put bounds to her immo-
derate fervour, as it seemed to them; but afterwards, seeing there could be no doubt but that
God concurred miraculously to support her, no
longer dared to make any opposition.

For the purpose of exciting in herself that
implacable hatred against her body, Mary Ann
availed herself of the thought of death, which
she had continually present. Among the other
articles, with which her new apartment was provided, there was, as we said before, a coffin. It
contained a wooden skeleton, dressed in the poor
habit of a Franciscan, having for a head, a real
human skull. It was exposed in the middle of
the first room, with a small crucifix·upon its
breast, and with two candles, which were always
kept burning. Before this lively image of
death the blessed soul passed long hours in profound meditation, considering the shortness of
life, the vanity of the things of the world, and
the state to which she would be reduced after
death: and hence she animated herself to greater
fervour and contempt of herself. The medita-

tion being over, which was always new to her,
she rose to her feet, and sprinkling the skeleton
with holy water, she said, "May God forgive
you, Mary Ann : which of the two will be your
lot—death eternal, or life everlasting?" She
repeated the same words every time she left or
entered her apartment, and prayed those who
very rarely came to visit her to do the same,
telling them, that she was the dead person there
exposed.   At night she never went to take her
brief repose, before sprinkling the skeleton with
holy water, repeating always the same words.
Besides this, she caused a small picture to be
painted, representing the head of a young lady,
one half of whose face was fresh, handsome and
pleasing, and the other half disfigured, putrid,
and full of vermin.   She kept it suspended from
the wall, near her own room ; and in it, as in a
mirror, contemplating the frailty of all exterior
beauty, she drew fresh courage to beautify her
soul every day with the garb of virtue, and to
maltreat her body, which would one day be reduced to a mass of worms and corruption.

For many years she observed, with the greatest exactness, the order prescribed for the different actions of the day, in the distribution of

time which she gave to Father Camaccio, her
first confessor. In it were assigned, counting
the day and night, five hours for mental prayer,
two disciplines, hair-shirts every day, and four
hours only reserved for sleep. Her fervour increasing with her years, she sketched with her
own hand another form of life, which, after it
was approved of by Brother Ferdinand della
Croce, her spiritual director, she continued to
observe to her death. I shall faithfully trans-
scribe it here, taking it from the juridical process, where it was inserted word for word; and
it is as follows:—

"At four o'clock in the morning I will get up,
and take the discipline, kneeling down, and I
will return thanks to the Lord, and recall to
mind the points of my meditation on the passion
of Jesus Christ. From four o'clock to half-past
five, mental prayer. From half-past five till six,
reflection: I will put on my hair-shirts and recite the canonical hours as far as none; I will
make my general and particular examens, and
go to the church. From half-past six to seven,
I will go to confession. From seven to eight,
during the time of one mass, I will prepare the
dwelling-place in my heart for the reception of

my Spouse. After receiving him, I will return
thanks to the Eternal Father for having given
me his Son, and offer him up to him, asking
many graces in return. From eight to nine, I
will pray to gain the indulgences for the souls
in purgatory. From nine to ten, I will recite
the five mysteries of the Rosary of the Blessed
Virgin Mary. At ten, during the time of one
mass, I will recommend myself to my patron
saints; but on Sundays and Festivals, I will
continue this exercise till eleven. After this, if
I stand in need of it, I will take some refreshment. At two in the afternoon, I will recite
vespers, and make the general and particular
examen. From two to five, some manual labour,
raising my heart to God, making frequent acts
of love. From five to six, spiritual reading;
and I will say complin. From six to nine, mental prayer, renewing the presence of God with
more attention. From nine to ten, I will leave
my room to go and get a glass of water, and
take some little and allowable recreation. From
ten to twelve, mental prayer. At midnight, the
life of some saint, as my spiritual reading, for
an hour; after that, I will say matins. From
an hour after midnight to four o'clock, I will

take my repose, Fridays upon my cross, the other nights upon my ladder; and before going to take any rest, I will first take the discipline. In time of Advent and Lent, on Mondays, Wednesdays, and Fridays, I will make my prayer from ten to twelve at night, on the cross. On Fridays, I will, moreover, place peas in my shoes, wear a crown made of thistles, and wrap a bandage, made of the same material, six times round my body; and I will fast the whole week, without tasting a morsel of any thing. On Sundays, I will take an ounce of bread; and every day communicate with the grace of God."

From this minute distribution of hours, every one sees that Mary Ann had not a moment of time left, that was not spent either in praising God, or mortifying herself. The routine of her life consisted in lengthy prayers, short and broken sleep, rigid fasts continued for whole weeks, frequent disciplines, daily hair-shirts, and other strange penitential contrivances. If we were not certain that in all this she was manifestly guided by the Spirit of God, we would be at a loss to discover how to excuse her of a want of moderation. And yet, she not only persevered constantly for so many years in

this rigorous course of life, without any abate-
ment, except sometimes when commanded by her
confessor, but so great was the insatiable desire
which she had of suffering, that she often took
occasion to add more and more to her austerities. A bit of paper was found after her death,
on which she wrote thus to her confessor:
"Father, should it please your Reverence to
give me permission, I would like to increase the
ordinary penances this Advent. I will use my
cross every night from six to seven o'clock; and
on Mondays, Wednesdays, and Fridays, put peas
in my shoes. Take the discipline every night
at eleven, one and four in the morning. Use
bandages of thistles every day; and a rough
covering, made of cords of bristles also, to macerate the arms and thighs, and a pointed iron
chain with four rows of links, for the sides; and
this, with the grace of God, from the Vigil of
All Saints to Easter. As to my fasts, I will
follow the rule which my spiritual Father left
me, of taking food only when necessity compels.
Father, let your Reverence determine whether
or not I have to practise any of these things
over and above what has been prescribed me.
Let your Reverence consult his Divine Majesty,

who will suggest what is pleasing to him; meanwhile, I do not desire aught than that Mary Ann
may be perfectly agreeable in the eyes of his
Divine Majesty; and the Lord grant, that this
be to his greater glory." This was signed with
her own hand.

But to descend more to particulars in this
matter. Mary Ann was in the habit, for many
years, of scourging herself five times every day,
counting day and night together; and she would
have exceeded this number of times, had she not
been restrained by her confessor. She used
different sorts of instruments, such as small
cords knotted together, or with little stars of
steel attached to the end; chains, with hooks
and iron points; little bundles of sharp and
stinging grass. Her manner was without any
moderation, or compassionate regard for herself;
fervour, not time, was her regulator; and with
such a strength of arm, that the walls and pavement around her were sprinkled with the blood
from her mangled flesh. In order to conceal
from the eyes of others the marks of blood
which were every day increased, she would call
her youngest nieces, and beg them to assist her
to wash the walls and pavement with hot water.

But afterwards, being afraid that they come to know at last the true cause of so much blood being scattered about, she no longer availed herself of their assistance, but of some servants of the house, to whom she also secretly gave her blood-stained clothes to be washed.

Among these servants, there was one by the name of Catharine, who far surpassed all the rest in stupidity and rudeness. She had very little understanding, but was a simple, good-natured creature, and therefore just the one to suit Mary Ann's purposes, who proposed to make use of her, not only to conceal, but increase the rigours of her penance. Having called her one day to come to her, she put a discipline in her hand, asking her, for the love of God, to do her the favour of assisting her to scourge herself. Catharine, stupid as she was, refused at first to do it, saying that she could never be induced to strike her own mistress. But the other used so many reasons, prayers, and supplications, that at last, offering violence to her own feelings, she was persuaded to humour her, thinking she was doing her a favour. After this, Mary Ann took her every day to her room, and modestly uncovering her shoulders, submitted them to

Catharine's blows. When this had been done
for some time, the good Indian one day, moved
to pity, threw the discipline down, and asked
her mistress leave to depart, as she had not
courage to continue that cruel torture. But the
servant of God, far from showing herself satisfied, became more earnest in her petitions to her
to continue, without any regard for her; and
when entreaties would not succeed, she had recourse to very ingenious arguments, telling her
to be under no fear of doing her harm, as she
perhaps believed. On the contrary, that by
complying with her wishes, she would procure
her the greatest possible good, by assisting her
to acquire more merits in this life, and consequently to reach a higher degree of glory in
paradise, where, once arrived, she would remember her as having been formerly the instrument and cause of such happiness. These
reasons, urged by her in a suppliant and en-
dearing manner, were sufficient to induce the
obtuse Catharine to continue without mercy the
cruel butchery, and to renew it every day, at the
discretion and pleasure of her young mistress.

In consequence of this severe and continued
ill-treatment, which Mary Ann either inflicted

on herself or by the hands of others, her shoulders were almost always covered with wounds: nor did she cease, therefore, to re-open and irritate the old wounds every day by fresh ones. And in order that all sense of pain might not be deadened by frequent repetition, in place of disciplines she substituted hair-cloths, which were like the bandages they use to dress incisions opened in the flesh by whips. More than thirty of these instruments of torture were found in her apartment after her death, and the whole of them were frightful to look at, both on account of the material, and the way they were made. Some of them were woven of rough bristles, others of sharp thistles, some, again, were like a coat of mail, studded with sharp iron points. There was no part of her body, we may say, to which she did not apply some special torture. For the head she had two crowns—one of thistles, and the other of iron, armed with sharp points; and she wore sometimes one, and sometimes the other, but in such a manner as not to be visible. For this purpose, when her head was shaved, she left in front two long locks of hair, and with them she strove to cover over and hide the crown from the eyes of others. She was not, however, always successful; for the blood oozing from the wounds of her head, and trickling down her face, betrayed her. Thus, it happened, for instance, when her nieces and some ladies once entered her apartment to take her with them to church, she came out with her face covered with many and small drops of fresh blood, which ran from under her hair. The ladies, frightened at the sight, anxiously enquired the cause; and she, modestly blushing, without answering a word, immediately re-entered her chamber, and after effacing the spots, returned with a smiling countenance, as if nothing at all was the matter. She had also two instruments of torture made like a jacket with sleeves—one of rough bristles, the other of little cords, with points of iron; but this last she was not permitted to wear, except on Fridays, and on the vigils of the festivals of her patron saints, which were many in the course of the year. Not unfrequently, she used to wear a dress likewise armed with sharp points, which extended from her neck almost down to her very feet. The pain which it caused her was intolerable, being unable either to move, sit, or kneel, with-

out being stung and pierced in every part of her
body. Around her neck, and extending over
her breast, she was accustomed sometimes to
wind an iron chain studded with sharp points in
four distinct folds. For her arms, besides the
bandages mentioned before, she had two sleeves
interwoven with sharp thistles; two little chains
of iron for each arm, or little cords of bristles,
which were tied so tightly round the flesh, that
for a long time afterwards the arm remained so
benumbed, that she lost all use of it. To torment her sides, she used not less than fifteen instruments of torture, of various forms, and all
of the roughest description. Ten of them,
although worn out, from the long use made of
them, were taken away from her by her confessor, because they were too excessively painful. Finally, she covered the inside soles of
her shoes with a coating of wax, and then inserted in it small stones, or dried peas; and
these she used every Monday, Wednesday, and
Friday of the week, going and returning from
her home to the church, and suffering, at every
step, the most excruciating pains in the soles of
her feet.

She could not certainly employ, at the same

time, all these dreadful instruments of penance;
nevertheless, those of every day were such, and
so numerous, that were we not certain that she
was directed and supported in a special manner
by God, who wished to give to the world in this
his servant an admirable example of innocence
and austerity, we could not excuse her of indis-
cretion and the height of excess. Catharine,
the Indian servant, who had the best opportunity of knowing her, testified on oath, in the
juridical process, that she was in the habit of
using every day not less than nine of these instruments of torture, sometimes many, or all, at
the same time, and again changing them in routine, in order to feel the pain more sensibly by
the variety and change of torture. And Father
Fra. Girolamo de Paredes, a Religious of the
holy order of St. Francis, and brother to Mary
Ann, was accustomed to say that his sister
always carried about her person more than
twenty pounds of iron; so many were the hair-
shirts, the chains, big and little, and the other
implements of penance with which, we may say,
her whole body was bound and laced. And yet
she was of a very weak and delicate constitution, and often afflicted with severe and painful

diseases, which, especially in the last eight years
of her life, were accompanied with the most
acute pains. Notwithstanding all this, she never
abated the smallest particle of her daily austerities, except when she was obliged to take to
her bed, or compelled, by order of her confessor.

Besides her ordinary mortifications, she had
her extraordinary ones for certain days and
times; which only her ardent and never-satiated
love of suffering could have suggested to her
mind. Being tenderly devoted, as she was, to
the passion of Jesus Christ, she studied by all
means possible to copy in herself the dreadful
pains and sufferings which the Redeemer un-
derwent whilst here on earth for our salvation.
Not content with what she had undertaken to do
from her childhood upon every Friday of the
year—which day was consecrated in a special
manner to the memory of the passion of Christ,
and which we have already related—from the
time she began to lead a solitary life, she gave
full scope to her fervour and love, adding other
unusual and painful austerities. She caused a
huge cross of wood to be made, and fastened at
the extremities of its arms and foot a certain
number of loops, something like handcuffs,

formed of cords made of very rough and slender
bristles; and having fastened it securely to the
wall, she crucified herself upon it every Friday
of the year. Having first put on the crown of
iron armed with sharp points, she approached
the cross with the greatest reverence, and getting upon a little stool, she first fastened the few
locks of hair, which we mentioned she had left
on the front part of her head to conceal the
crown, to some little cords hanging from the
top of the cross; after this, with considerable
difficulty, she inserted first the hands, and then
the feet, into the loops of thistle bristles, and
pushing away the stool from under her feet, she
remained suspended, with the whole weight of
her body supported by these five bands, and in
this state she continued two and three hours at
a time, absorbed in God, and meditating the
passion of her heavenly Spouse. Afterwards,
in time of Lent and Advent, besides Fridays,
she placed herself upon the cross also on Mondays and Wednesdays; and very often on Satur-
days, to commemorate the dolours of the Most
Blessed Virgin. What is more, whilst she hung
thus suspended, she entreated her servant Catharine, as a great favour, to press hard upon

and force down the crown; and the consequence was, her head became, as it were, one wound, and the bristles encircling the ancles and wrists being drawn tighter, broke the skin, and tore the flesh. Her strength was completely exhausted under this dreadful torture, and as her servant Catharine attested, she was unable to move, much less to stand upon her feet, for many hours afterwards.

But the more she suffered, the more she always desired to suffer to become more and more conformable to the image of her crucified Saviour. She would have wished to give her life and blood in testimony and token of her love; and therefore not being satisfied with lacerating her flesh with so many instruments of penance, once a week, and if she could, on Fridays, under pretence that her frequent maladies required it, she caused them to open a vein and bleed her. But whatever pretence she alleged, those of the house knew very well, that it was nothing else than a desire of shedding her blood for Jesus Christ. Nor could she herself, although very cautious and guarded, on more occasions than one conceal it, the joy and delight which she felt were visible upon her face. It happened on one

occasion when the surgeon had performed the
operation, and was about closing the vein by
bandaging the arm, Mary Ann being suddenly
seized by one of those transports of love, with
which her soul was inflamed, drawing back her
arm, begged him to allow her ignoble and
worthless blood to flow, since Jesus Christ, her
spouse, had shed his own most precious blood
in much greater quantity for such a miserable
sinner as she was. When afterwards this occurred on Good-Friday, the joy she felt was
indescribable. Having been attacked one year
by a fever on that day, the attending physician
ordered her to be bled. The announcement
visibly affected her, and, unable to restrain the
ardour of her joy, she exclaimed—let infinite
thanks be given to God. who has deigned to
allow me on this day to shed a small quantity
of blood. The fact would be incredible, were
it not certified in the process by several ocular
witnesses and persons of standing: viz., that in
little over a year she was bled one hundred and
sixty times. The family marvelled, and the
physicians and surgeons were still more astonished; and they declared, that, according to the
laws of nature, it was impossible, considering

the scantiness of the diet which Mary Ann, as
we saw, was accustomed to take every eight or
fifteen days, such an abundance of blood should
be produced.

And that God really was the agent here, was
plainly to be seen from many signs and prodi
gies. Martino della Pegna, a learned physician
and a man of known probity, made an agreement with Mary Ann, that he would cure in her
the maladies which afflicted her body, provided
she would obtain of Almighty God, by her
prayers, a cure for a depression of spirits under
which he laboured. Having obtained the favour
for which he had asked, it cannot be expressed
with what care and solicitude he applied himself to her every want. Having paid her a visit
one day, and it was the Good-Friday of 1645,
he found her with such a burning fever that he
judged it necessary for her to be bled; and
without waiting for a surgeon, he himself, on
the spot, opened a vein. But what was his
surprise, when he saw a thin stream of clear and
limpid water first spirt from the incision, and
then after some time fresh blood follow? As
tonished at the novelty of the thing, he could
not refrain from saying, Miss, such a thing as

this never happened except in the side of the
Redeemer. Mary Ann made him no answer;
and only a modest blush suffused her face. When
the vein was closed, a small fleshy excrescence
was formed in the scar, which protruded like
the head of a nail; and it lasted till her death,
causing her a severe pain, as if something sharp
was always piercing her arm in that particular
spot. D. Maria della Rosa was present, together with several other ladies, and having a
great opinion of Mary Ann's sanctity, unseen by
any one, dipped her linen handkerchief in the
blood, which seemed to her miraculous, and
when she was returned to her own home, wished
to see it; but to her great surprise, she perceived her handkerchief just as white and clean
as when it first came from the wash.

The blessed servant of God having discovered
that some persons sought after her blood to
preserve it, gave orders to her Indian servant,
Catharine, that whenever she was bled she
should throw the blood in the garden attached
to the house, that the earth might absorb every
trace of it. The servant complied in part with
her orders, but not entirely; because having
dug a little hole in a distant and less frequented

corner. she regularly deposited in it her mistress' blood. and then closed the mouth of the hole with a stone. After some time her curiosity was excited to know how it was preserved there; and with a little stick in her hand she began to stir the blood in the hole, and found it as fresh and uncorrupt as if it had just been extracted from the vein. Surprised at this, and hardly believing her own eyes, she returned very often, and at different times and years, to try the same experiment, and always found the blood perfectly pure; wherefore full of wonder, she could not refrain from telling her mistress of it, with her usual simplicity, who gave her no other answer than these words: "Blessed be the Lord; that the blood of Mary Ann, a sinner, remains without being corrupted. This prodigy continued till after Mary Ann's death: or rather God then confirmed it by another more singular and remarkable prodigy, which we will give in its proper place.

CHAPTER VII.

THE EXTRAORDINARY RIGOUR PRACTISED BY THE
BLESSED MARY ANN, IN THE SHORT SLEEP WHICH
SHE TOOK DURING THE NIGHT. DESCRIPTION OF
HER ORDINARY AND EXTRAORDINARY BEDS. HER
WONDERFUL ABSTINENCE FROM EVERY KIND OF
FOOD, PROLONGED FROM EIGHT TO FIFTEEN DAYS
IN SUCCESSION, AND RENDERED MORE PAINFUL
BY AN HEROIC EXERCISE OF MORTIFICATION.

THIS did not put an end to the evil treatment
with which this fervent virgin afflicted her innocent body during the whole course of her life.
Besides the torments which we have already
recounted, she added this of inflicting pain upon
herself during the night, curtailing her repose,
and by a thousand artifices and inventions, and
depriving herself of every necessary sustenance
by a strict fast prolonged for days and weeks.

And in the first place, as regards her sleep,
she had assigned in her distribution of time but
three hours of the night; and she gradually
diminished it afterwards so much, that, as Father

Camaccio her confessor attested, she reduced to
one hour only. But I am at a loss to say whether that brief space of time, which she gave
from necessity to repose, strictly speaking, deserves the name of sleep, and not rather that of
a prolonged torture. She had in one of her
rooms a little bed, poor it is true, but neat and
kept in good order, which served only for the
purpose of concealing her rigid austerities from
the eyes of others. She never used it unless
when compelled by obedience of her confessor,
or in case only of severe indisposition. The
ordinary bed, however, on which she lay was a
ladder of a triangular form, with the bars not
rounded, but made rough, shapeless and pointed.
One evening her Indian servant, Catharine,
being left alone in her room, chanced to see this
strange bed, which had been drawn out from its
place of concealment, where her mistress generally kept it during the day, and which now
stood prepared for use in her room; and wishing to know with what convenience one could lie
upon it, stretched herself upon it at full length.
In this position Mary Ann unexpectedly surprised her, and with a sweet smile said to her—
" Ah, well—is my bed soft and nice enough for

you?" To whom the servant, with her usua'
simplicity, replied—"It is a real instrument of
torture, and my bones are already aching, al
though I was on it only for a moment: and you.
my Lady, can you really sleep upon this dreadful
rack?" "Yes," "replied the servant of God, "I
sleep upon it; I tell you, moreover, that this is
one of Mary Ann's delights. We have to do
and suffer some little thing in order to merit
and gain heaven: and when I consider the im-
mensity that my Divine Spouse has done and
suffered for me, what I do and suffer for him
appears to me as nothing."

But this ladder caused her no little suffering
during the whole course of her life. To D. Giovanna, her niece, to whom her confessor once
obliged her to give an account of her interiour,
she candidly confessed, that of an evening, when
she was about to extend herself upon the ladder,
her heart was so oppressed, and she felt such a
repugnance and horror, that not unfrequently
she fell into violent swoons and deadly sweats.
At the thought alone, that upon that hard bed
she would never be able to close an eye, and
that she would rise from it with her body all
bruised and pained, and this not for one or two

nights, but for the rest of her days, as long as
she had health and strength, she said she felt,
every time, as if she were seized by the agonies
of death; so great was the repugnance of the
flesh to the spirit. Notwithstanding all this,
rather than succumb or yield an inch to her
feelings, she became more generous and courageous to blunt her every emotion of natural repugnance.   The more she felt herself assailed
by it, the more violently she threw herself upon
that pile of wood, and rolling herself upon it
with the whole weight of her body, she spoke in
a loud voice to herself, "Aha, Mary Ann, do
you feel uneasiness and pain upon this bed?
Complain as much as you please: your Spouse
has suffered much more than you.   Have you a
feeling of pain and torment?   Enjoy it a thousand times: you have deserved greater chastisements for your sins."   Nor was she yet satisfied: after having been for some time upon the
ladder, she got up and wrapt herself in a kind
of thick mat made of bristles, and shaped like a
bag, the inside of which was filled with small
sharp and cutting stones, and continuing to talk
to her afflicted body, she said to it, "Be quiet
now, and comfort yourself: you were anxious

to enjoy delights, ease, and soft linen; and here
is every thing together, in this covering sheet,
which the nicest art can invent for your convenience. Wrap yourself well up in it, enjoy
its softness, and take your pleasure till you are
satisfied in the convenience of the bed which
you desire." In this manner did this innocent
and delicate young girl punish in herself as
faults the repugnance which was but natural.
Let so many delicate and effeminate young ladies
look upon this model and example, and be con-
founded, who cannot suffer the roughness of a
dress, the puncture of a needle, and whose
whole time and attention is taken up in pam-
pering and caressing their body, although always
opposed and rebellious to the spirit, and in
shunning the slightest suffering and the most
trifling mortification. And yet, without this, it
is very difficult to keep the passions in subjection, and to remove the obstacles and dangers
which are to be met with in the way of salvation. But let us return to Mary Ann.

We have seen what was her ordinary bed.
She had also extraordinary ones, for certain
times; casting herself, often in the depth of
winter, to sleep upon the bare ground, with a

rough piece of wood, or a hard stone, under her
head for a pillow, and stretching herself upon a
most curious instrument of torture of her own
invention, which was transferred, after her death,
to the College of the Fathers of the Society of
Jesus, where it is preserved with the greatest
veneration. This was a log of wood sufficiently
large and of a round form, into which she fastened one hundred and seven of the sharpest
kind of thorns, at an equal distance from each
other, in such a manner, that in what position
soever the servant of God would lie, she was
sure to have her flesh cruelly pierced on every
side. She generally lay on this piece of torture
every Friday of the year, after having first suffered a martyrdom on the other, which was
erect and standing against the wall, which we
have already described. At other times, carried
away by the violence of her fervour, she would
run to embrace and press it to her bosom, tearing her breast with the thorns, and covering
the log with the blood which flowed from the
wounds and which, for many years after her
death, remained as fresh and as red as ever.

She used also to go and sleep in the coffin
which she kept in her apartment, after deposit-

ing the skeleton on the ground; as also to extend herself, naked, upon a bed made of the
stems of nettles. This she called her soft and
delicious bed: and such it was in reality for
the soul, for which sufferings, both interior as
well as exterior, were a solace; but not so for
the body, which left that bed of thorns all
pierced and bloody—for in that part of South
America, the nettles are not, as with us, a small
delicate little plant with a slender stem, but
they grow to a great height, and have long and
solid trunks, as thick as a man's fist, which
shoot out strong and long thorns all over them.
There was one of her more trusted servants,
who, from time to time, as she received orders,
purchased these plants, and after stripping them
of their leaves, brought by night the naked and
thorny stems into Mary Ann's rooms, who afterwards arranged and fixed them to suit herself.
And she was just precisely preparing, one evening, this dreadful bed of torture, when, believing she was not heard by any one, she began to
talk to herself in a loud voice, " Well, does
Mary Ann, then, wish to sleep upon a soft and
convenient bed? Very well. I'll give her the
bed which she deserves." Catharine, the Indian

servant. was in the next room, who, hearing her
mistress talk in this manner, immediately guess-
ed what it was. But, without this, she discovered it many times the next morning, when,
being obliged, according to the argreement with
Mary Ann, secretly to carry away these things
and bury them under ground in the domestic
garden, she found them all crushed and be-
smeared with blood.

Nor was the abstinence less wonderful and
out of the usual course of nature, which the
Blessed Mary Ann of Jesus practised during the
whole term of her mortal career. All the witnesses who testified in the different processes,
agreed in saying, that God, by a continued
miracle, preserved the life of his servant for
more than twenty-six years; it being impossible
that nature could, without the aid of supernatural help, support herself, I will not say for a
year, nor a month, but a few days only, on such
slight and scanty nourishment, which might be
called rather the appearance than a substantial
food. We have seen how, whilst she was still
in her infancy, and a little girl of but few years,
she began to fast with such rigour that frequently she would fall into mortal swoons and

fainting fits from extreme weakness; extending
her fasts to twenty-four hours at a time, without
tasting a morsel of bread. Nor did she relax
any thing of her fasts as she advanced in years:
on the contrary, she was always curtailing and
reducing her allowance of food. She had hardly
attained the use of reason when she abstained
altogether from flesh, and not long after also
from any thing composed either of milk or eggs,
and from fish, and from every other kind of food
that was any ways substantial or delicate. And
in this she was so constant and firm, then even
in her severe attacks of illness, it was not possible to induce her to taste any other food; the
Almighty concurring in a wonderful manner to
render every other food not only disagreeable
to the taste, but injurious to the stomach, except what was her ordinary and common diet.
Her confessors very often commanded her to
break this law of rigorous fast in the quality as
well as the quantity of her food : and she, perfectly obedient to their wish, acquired the full
merit of obedience, although at the cost of unspeakable suffering, for she was never able to
retain upon her stomach or derive any sustenance from the foods prescribed her: the conse-

quence was, they had to revoke the order, in order not to aggravate her pains and afflictions, and endanger her life.

One time when she was sick, Father Monosalvas, of the Society of Jesus, who was at that time her confessor, went to visit her. He found her very emaciated and feeble; and believing this arose from a want of proper nourishment, ordered her, on the spot, to take three fresh eggs. The Blessed Mary Ann, with the true spirit of interiour submission, suppressing every natural repugnance, without offering a word of excuse, in the presence of the Father, took the eggs, and with an heroic act of resignation swallowed them down, although she foresaw the excruciating torture which they would undoubtedly cause her. It seemed, however, that this time she would be able to retain them, and that they would do her good; for after having swallowed them she remained perfectly quiet and calm and Father Monosalvas returned to the college, well pleased that he had been so successful in making her take that little nourishment with such happy result. But he had hardly set his foot outside the house before the servant of God was immediately seized with violent

convulsions and dreadful contortions in her
stomach, which, for three successive days, allowed her not a moment of rest or repose. She
could without doubt easily have rid herself of
her misery by discharging at once the food from
her stomach, which she was unable to digest,
but for fear of being wanting in obedience she
preferred to suffer with invincible constancy
this lengthy torment. At the end of three days
her confessor returned to pay her another visit;
and having asked her about the state of her
health, she told him plainly of the great sufferings she had endured during his absence, and
humbly asked his permission to vomit. Having
obtained it, she immediately threw up the yolks
of the three eggs as sound and entire as she had
taken them three days before, to the astonishment of all present, who could not observe the
slightest change produced on them by the action
of the stomach during all that time.

Another time a plain cup of chocolate was presented to her by a lady, an intimate friend. She
at first very politely declined it; but being
pressed and importuned with many entreaties
and prayers, was at length induced to take a
few sips. And behold, at that very instant she

is assailed with acute pains in her bowels and
violent contortions in her stomach, from which
she is only relieved after throwing up with much
suffering the little nourishment she tasted. More
singular still is the fact, which I will here relate, copying it faithfully from the process.   D.
Sebastiana di Casso and Catharine, the Indian
servant, both of whom lodged in Mary Ann's
apartments, made an agreement one day together
that they would secretly prepare a dish a little
better seasoned: and that the servant of God
might have no pretext for refusing it, they neither used flesh, fish nor milk in its composition.
They then made a savoury ragout, composed
entirely of common and ordinary herbs; but
with such precaution that it was the same in
appearance and smell as the ordinary food the
Saint was accustomed to take.   The simple Indian, however, could not refrain from telling her
mistress that D. Sebastiana had that day wished
to prepare the food for her.   To whom Mary
Ann smiling replied—" I am very much obliged
to her for her charity; but I foresee that she
will make it such that I shall not be able to
taste it."   Catharine assured her that the food
was perfectly Lenten, and that it contained

nothing of those things which she refused. "And yet," added the other, "you will see that I shall not be able to take it." Both of them came together, at the usual hour, into Mary Ann's room, and set before her the dish of herbs. But she had no sooner seen it than pushing it from her with horror—"Did I not tell you," she exclaimed, "that your labour would be useless? Why do you wish that I should eat meat to-day, when you know, that both on account of the law of abstinence, and the weakness of my stomach, I cannot taste of such foods?" At these words the two women looked at each other, perfectly bewildered, and lost in amazement at the novelty of the prodigy, by which, at that very instant, the herbs were converted into flesh, and were unable to utter a word. From this they were finally convinced, that it was the will of Almighty God she should never change in the least her way of abstinence: and the consequence was, that neither they nor any of the house, not even her confessors themselves, ever afterwards, dared to solicit her to moderate any thing of her rigour.

Even from her tender years, her whole diet consisted of a very small quantity of cabbage boiled simply in water, and without any season-

iug, not even salt. When she was eight years
of age, she deprived herself also of this; satisfied to support herself on a little bread and
water. She fasted rigorously three days in the
week, and on all the vigils of the Most Blessed
Virgin and her patron saints. Besides the ordinary Lent prescribed by the Church, which
she called the Fast of the Holy Passion, she
added two others of much longer duration—one
from Easter to Pentecost, called also, by her,
the Glorious Fast; and the third, from the vigil
of All Saints to the solemnity of Christmas.
During all this time she took but a limited
allowance of bread and water, and this only
once a day. When she had completed her
eleventh year, she carried her abstinence so far
as to pass four entire days, from the Wednesday
of Holy Week to noon of Easter Sunday, without food or drink. Thenceforward, as if all her
abstinence heretofore had been but experiments
of childish fervour, she fasted so vigorously,
that, as we find it recorded in the juridical process, she only took food every fifteen days, and
then but a small slice of bread, which her
stomach again rejected, after retaining it a
short time. Such was her way of living for

many years; until, on account of her severe in-
dispositions, she was compelled by her confessor
to take more frequent nourishment. From this
time she was induced to break her fast every
eight days, but she never took any thing but a
small slice of bread, which never amounted to
more than an ounce. D. Scolastica Sarmiento
testified to having seen in Mary Ann's rooms
several of those little cakes which they are accustomed to bless on the Feast of St. Nicholas,
and that they were so small, that, perhaps, the
whole of them together would hardly weigh a
single ounce. A single one of these, was the
only nourishment she took every eight days.
So that, during the whole time of Lent, she was
not accustomed to eat but six ounces of bread,
and four in Advent—that is to say, an ounce
every Sunday; and with this scanty allowance
she not unfrequently mixed, for her greater
mortification, ashes, or gall, and sometimes bitter herbs, to render it as unpleasant as possible
to the taste. It was to be feared, moreover,
that her throat would become so contracted
from the want of moisture, that her life was endangered from suffocation, and then she was obliged to remedy the evil by sipping water, or

keeping in her mouth a small piece of quince, and gradually extracting its juice. Finally, in the last years of her life, it can be said in all truth, that she derived no support whatever from natural food, because even that small particle of food, which she took every eight days, and the juice of the quince, which she swallowed once in every eighteen or twenty days, she was unable to retain on her stomach, but soon rejected, almost as soon as she took it.

In order to render her extraordinary abstinence still more painful, and to stifle with heroic mortification every temptation to gluttony, she was in the habit, as long as she was in good health, of serving her relations at table, and in this manner, by the sight of the dainty dishes before her, to make her own want more keenly sensible. At first, her brother-in-law and sister were strongly opposed to it, for their hearts could not endure the sight of that little angel acting the part of a servant every day at table. But she begged so hard, and brought forward so many reasons, that at last, for fear of giving her pain, they dared not longer oppose her. After some time, however, there was not one of the family who was not displeased that such a thing should be tolerated; for which reason, D. Cosimo hit upon the expedient of changing every day the hour of dining, thinking, by this means, to escape the vigilance of Mary Ann. But it was all useless; for no sooner had they sat down to table, than Mary Ann always made her appearance with a smile upon her face, and ready to discharge her humble office. It would frequently happen that her sister, or some one of the guests, who were aware of her abstinence, would offer her something to eat; but it was never possible to induce her to taste even so much as a mouthful, and she knew how to excuse herself in such cases with such a good grace, and with so much civility in her words and manner, that she gained the love and veneration of all present. She wished, however, that her portion should be preserved untouched; but it was only that she might relieve, with it, a poor Indian woman, whom she charitably supplied every day with food. When dinner was over, and there was nothing more to be done, she suggested some pious sentiment to the guests, and then, taking her departure, retired to her solitude, leaving all present edified with her humility and mortification.

The fame of Mary Ann's extraordinary abstinence being spread over the city, every one was loud in praise of her wonderful sanctity. There was no condition or class of persons that were not of opinion that her rigid course of life was more than natural, and that God undoubtedly concurred to support her with virtue more than human. The more, as every one remembered the frequent and cruel disciplines she took, the continual and horrible hair-cloths she always bore about her person, the daily loss of so much blood occasioned by bloody disciplines, or the punctures of iron chains and thorns, or drawn by the surgeon, her short and unpleasant sleep, so many years spent without the enjoyment of any solace or recreation, as also her long prayers and meditations on her knees, and the continual guard she kept over her senses, the contradictions she always offered to her own will, they were at a loss to understand how a small slice of bread and a few sips of water, taken so sparingly and afterwards rejected, could naturally afford that amount of strength as would be required not to sink, irreparably oppressed and overcome, under the weight of such austerity, as would have been insupportable to a man of the strongest and most robust constitution, but much more so to a delicate girl, and one so young, of a noble family, of a very feeble constitution, and almost always sick.

It is almost inconceivable how insupportable to the humility of the servant of God were the opinion and praises of men. She would have wished that none knew or spoke of her; and consequently she made use of every art and exertion to hide her fasts from the eyes of others, even at the cost of great inconveniences and sufferings. One of the principal ladies of the city, giving little credit to the general belief that was current of the extraordinary abstinence of Mary Ann, wished to be convinced of it with her own eyes, and therefore having gone one morning to pay her a visit, took the liberty to tell her that she would remain and dine with her. The Saint, in the kindest manner, expressed her happiness to have her company, and suspecting perhaps the cause, gave orders to have her table well supplied that day, and eat herself of several dishes. But no sooner was the lady gone, than she had to discharge from her stomach, with much pain, every thing she had taken. At other times she would order her

servant Catharine to make her some nice and
delicate dishes, and afterwards make her carry
them, openly and in sight of every body, into
her apartment.　She hoped by this to make the
family and strangers believe she occasionally
indulged in better diet.　But the Indian, with
her usual simplicity, betrayed her; for as much
as she was distinguished for her obedience, so
much the more solicitous she was to disclose to
others that her mistress, without tasting the
dishes that were brought her, gave the whole
of them to the poor.

CHAPTER VIII.

THE BLESSED MARY ANN, AFTER BEING REDUCED
TO THE LAST DEGREE OF ATTENUATION BY THE
RIGOUR OF HER FASTS, IS INSTANTANEOUSLY
RESTORED TO HER USUAL APPEARANCE AND
STRENGTH, WHICH MIRACULOUSLY CONTINUES
TO HER DEATH. PROOFS OF HER BEING SUP-
PORTED FOR MANY YEARS ON DAILY COMMUNION
ALONE. HER TENDER DEVOTION TO THE MOST
BLESSED SACRAMENT OF THE ALTAR.

But what afflicted the blessed child most, was
the extenuation and meagerness to which, from
the beginning, she was reduced. Her face was
pale and without colour, every member of her
body emaciated and withered, so that she had
more the appearance of a skeleton, covered with
a thin skin, than a real and sound body. This
exteriour appearance, which it was impossible
to conceal, gave her no little uneasiness, as it
betrayed to every body's eyes the natural effects
of her excessive rigours. Besides, her sister
and brother-in-law being much concerned at the

thought of losing her forever, had, for a long
time past, used argument and entreaties to in
duce her to abate something of that excessive ab
stemiousness, which had exhausted her strengtl
and attenuated her body. And when they saw
they lost their time in endeavouring to make
her alter her resolution, they applied to Fathe
John Camaccio, that he would use his authorit
as confessor, and oblige her in virtue of obe
dience to change her way of life, and save her
self from certain death. He, although he had
been inspired by Almighty God to approve he
way of living, yet afterwards seeing that with
out an evident miracle, she would not be able
to hold out much longer, was also inclined to
revoke or suspend the permission given her.

Things having reached this state, Mary An
found herself in the greatest perplexity and
agitation of mind. She had the clearest convic
tion by light infused into her mind from above
that the manner of her penance was pleasing to
her Divine Spouse; and in this she was certain
of not going astray. But on the other side hei
excessive paleness and leanness was the cause
of considerable anxiety to her, as it would affore
an occasion to the family of frequently renewing

their entreaties, and importuning her confessor
to forbid her every extraordinary rigour, and
would be also to strangers a reason and argument of thinking her a very mortified and penetential person, which to her humility was insupportable. Not knowing then what to do, she
shut herself up in her rooms, and redoubling
her prayers for many days, she prayed her heavenly Spouse that he would grant her the special
grace of leading a life in perfect conformity with
his most holy will, yet without any exteriour
show, wishing to live entirely unknown to the
eyes of men. After praying in this manner with
many tears, she felt an interiour voice which
told her that her prayer was heard. She went
early the next morning to the church of the
Jesuits, and having sent for Father Camaccis,
she told him that he should suspend his judgment for a little while in regard to her fasts:
that he should, before resolving, consult more
earnestly the will of Almighty God: that he
should say the mass of the Holy Ghost for her
that very morning, and implore light from heaven. The Father after hearing this went immediately to celebrate, and Mary Ann communicated with extraordinary fervour; then after

spending some considerable time in thanksgiving, she returned to the confessional to speak again to her director, and she had scarcely got on her knees before she was overpowered by a sweet sleep, something like an exstacy. A little after she returned to her senses and perceived herself suddenly quite an altered person. She was no longer pale and meagre, but florid and gay; her hands no longer dry and emaciated, but full and fleshy; her face fresh and rosy; her whole air and appearance were so exceedingly beautiful and resplendent, that she seemed like an angel just descended from heaven. The servant of God was herself sensible of the sudden change, and therefore turning to her confessor, "I believe, Father," said she, "there can be no longer a doubt as to the divine will." Father Camaccio was perfectly astonished at the miraculous change; and adoring the admirable dispensation of Almighty God, comforted Mary Ann, and exhorted her to continue the way of life she had began. Her relations also, as soon as they perceived the change wrought in her countenance, and that air of angelic beauty, which modestly shone in her face, congratulated themselves, believing that she had at last been induced to moderate somewhat the excessive rigour of her penances, especially in regard of fasting. But in the course of time, observing that she continued to mortify her body as she was previously accustomed to do, and to pass whole weeks without any nourishment, and yet always maintained the same state of florid health, which could not be impaired, even in appearance, by long sicknesses, to which she was subject, nor death itself, they reasonably suspected that this must be some supernatural or miraculous interposition of divine providence.

In proof of this also, there was another prodigy, not as visible as the first to the exteriour eye, but still equally certain and no less extraordinary. All who gave testimony in the different processes, either as eye-witnesses or who spoke to their own certain knowledge of Mary Ann's fasts, all without exception agreed in affirming, that by a special favour of Almighty God she lived for many years, and was entirely supported by that heavenly and spiritual food, which she received every day in holy communion, having no longer any need of material or earthly food. It was without doubt the same

singular and extraordinary grace that was form
erly conferred on St. Catharine of Sienna, St.
Rose of Lima, and several other favoured souls,
to whom Almighty God wished to assimilate the
Blessed Mary Ann, in the gratuitous distribution of supernatural gifts, as she had closely
resembled them in the innocence and austerity
of her life.

That she really lived on holy communion,
the testimony of Fathers John Camaccio, Antonio Monosalvas, and Alfoso Roxas, who, from
having been her confessors, were acquainted
with her every action, even the most insignifi-
cant, although hidden and interiour, leaves no
room for doubt. At the time that sudden storm
of contradictions was excited against the servant
of God,. on account of her daily communion,
which we have described in another place,
among the other reasons which Father Camaccio
brought forward in her defence before the
Bishop of Quito and the theologians deputed to
discuss and define the question, one was this:
that to forbid frequent communion to Mary
Ann, would be the same as to deny her the only
sustenance on which she lived. And that he
said the truth was also observable in the effects,

which were remarked by her relatives and those belonging to the house. For having been forbidden to approach the holy table whilst the matter was being discussed, Mary Ann became subject to great weakness and deadly swoons, and had hardly strength enough to stand upon her feet, which she immediately afterwards recovered as soon as she was allowed to receive every day. In the last years of her life it was so evident that the Eucharistic bread was her only food, that every one believed it, and it had ceased to be a matter of surprise.

It pleased Almighty God, that Mary Ann herself should, on more occasions than one, be unable to dissemble or deny this singular favour granted her by a special grace of heaven. One day she exhorted her Indian servant Catharine to fast on bread and water, for the love of Jesus: and the other replying " that she would do so willingly, if she were a Saint like herself;" "do what you can on your part," added the servant of the Lord, "and God will not be wanting with his assistance to give you health and strength to do it." The good servant smiled to hear her talk so; and I "began," she said, in her deposition, "to fast the best I could, but I could never equal my mistress." At another time the same Catharine, wondering very much at her great abstinence, took the liberty to ask Mary Ann "how in the world she managed to live, as she could not retain the little nourishment which she took every eight days, but had always almost immediately to reject it again?" Mary Ann, with a smile, told her that "every morning, when she left the house, she went to eat a live lamb, whole and entire, and of course she had no need of other food." The poor simple woman did not question the truth of what she said, nor understand the meaning of her words: rather considering, in her own mind, the answer of her mistress, resolved to keep watch and see in what place and what hour the victuals were secretly prepared. To carry out her plan, she got up very early for several days, and closely followed Mary Ann when she issued forth at day-break: and observing that the only way she took was to the church of the Jesuits, she came at length to the conclusion that the entire and living lamb, on which she fed, was the divine Sacrament of the Eucharist, which she received every day.

More explicit still was the declaration which

the Saint made to Petronilla of St. Byruns, a
lady of exalted piety and her confident, and who
afterwards became a nun in the monastery of St.
Clare. This lady having heard many persons
say that Mary Ann of Jesus lived on communion
alone, took the liberty which, that intimate
friendship which existed between them gave
her, to turn the conversation, when they were
talking together one day on heavenly things,
purposely on the most Blessed Sacrament, and
then plainly asked the servant of God if such
really were the effects which that divine food
produced in her: and she pressed and urged her
with so many questions and prayers, that at
length the other being overcome by her entreaties, candidly confessed that she no longer
needed natural food; that the holy Eucharist
was sufficient to support her life.

I will further add, that sometimes not only
communion, but the very hope of soon receiving
it was enough for Mary Ann to cure her perfectly of severe and dangerous corporal infirmities; and in proof of it I will relate a wonderful
fact, which I find recorded in the process. Father John Camaccio having left the city of Quito,
she took Father Antonio Monosalvas for her

confessor. This Father, who from not being
yet acquainted with her virtue, had been one
amongst the most strenuous opposers of daily
communion, no sooner saw her at his feet than
he forbade her to communicate the next day, as
she had desired and asked, it being the vigil of
St. John the Baptist, to whom she was very
devout. The humble servant of the Lord obeyed
without reply; but she was hardly returned
home, before she was assailed that very day
with a malignant fever, and accompanied with
such violence that the physicians, with all their
skill, could give her no relief, and in a short
time she was brought almost to death's door.
As soon as Father Monosalvas heard of it, he
went immediately to visit her, and fearing the
beginning of the disorder was no other than his
refusal to allow her to communicate when going
away, consoled her by telling her that he expected her the next morning in church, where
she would be able to receive the bread of angels. That was enough, for Mary Ann recovered immediately her health and strength. At
the first dawn of day she left the house, and so
eager was she to go to church, that she had to
wait some time outside the door till the church

was opened. Her confessor could scarcely believe his eyes when he first saw her, and asked her if it were her great desire of communicating that induced her to expose herself in that manner, and come at such an early hour, sick as she was. But being convinced by her reply and her looks that she was perfectly free of fever, and entirely cured, he was persuaded that the will of God was too clearly expressed for him to deprive that innocent and fervent soul any longer of that divine food, which is the bread and support of the strong.

Finally, the presence alone of the Eucharistic Sacrament was for Mary Ann the sweetest comfort which she could have on earth. She spent five or six hours of the day in the church of the Jesuits, and always motionless, with her eyes either fixed on the tabernacle or on the altars, in the act of profound adoration of the most Blessed Sacrament. Every year during both the three last days of Carnival and those of Holy Week she never left the church, even at night, but remained all the time without repose and without food, to keep company with her Beloved. She was sometimes seen with her face quite inflamed, and panting as it were with the

vehemence of her affection, unable to control
the flame of divine love which consumed her
inmost soul. At other times she remained as
one in an ecstacy, transported out of herself,
bereft entirely of her senses, and bathed in a
flood of tender tears, which quietly flowed from
her eyes. At this time she was perfectly insensible to all that passed around her, and it was
useless to call her even with a loud voice by her
name, or shake her by her dress or person, in
order to make her come to herself. Ocular
witnesses affirmed that there was frequently
about her, before and after communion, an air
of angelic beauty; that her face was surrounded
with rays, or resplendent with the brightest
light; that it dazzled the eyes of all who beheld
it. At which time it was useless to approach
her to speak to her, although it were only for a
moment and of necessary things. One morning
one of the Society went to her to tell her something of importance, some considerable time
after she had approached the holy table, whilst
she was still kneeling in a corner of the church,
with her veil drawn down over her breast, and
her mind wholly recollected in God. He called
her many times, but always without effect; be

cause she neither heard nor saw any thing. At
last coming to herself, she raised her head a
little, and with her face inflamed in an extraordinary manner, "My Father," said she, "I have
just finished my communion," and without another word she covered herself again, and continued her profound contemplation. Were we
to judge from what appeared exteriourly in her
person, what must we imagine must have been
the interiour delights which replenished her
soul. But we shall have an opportunity of
speaking of these more in detail in another
place. What has been said will suffice to show
us her extraordinary and wonderful love towards the divine Sacrament of the altar.

CHAPTER IX.

THE SOLITARY LIFE OF THE BLESSED MARY ANN IN
HER DOMESTIC RETREAT. HER INTERIOUR MOR-
TIFICATION AND PERFECT MASTERY OVER HER
PASSIONS. HOW PERFECTLY SHE OBSERVED HER
VOWS OF POVERTY AND OBEDIENCE EVEN IN
THINGS DIFFICULT AND REPUGNANT TO NATURE.

In taking up the history of the life of the
Blessed Mary Ann, it is but proper we should

speak of her domestic solitude, of her entire
detachment from every thing created. of the
denial of her own will, which are also parts of
the interiour as well as exteriour mortification,
of which we have been heretofore speaking.

From the moment the blessed child, at the
age of twelve, voluntarily shut herself up in her
retirement, she lived in the midst of the world,
within the walls of her paternal home, and in a
thickly crowded city, no otherwise than if she
had been in the most remote and forsaken solitude of the desert.   She no longer allowed any
one from without to enter her rooms, nay, not
even her nearest relatives of the house, except
very rarely, or on business; desiring to live
solely to herself, and completely aloof from the
world, which she had renounced forever.   The
day dedicated to the festival of the most Blessed
Trinity was the only exception, when her apartment was opened to those of the family, and
this only for the purpose of conducting them to
her little altar, there to pay their tribute of
adoration to that august mystery, to which she
was extremely devout. Before introducing them,
however, she set her poor furniture in good
order, washed the walls and pavements of the

spots of blood scattered over them, and hid all
her instruments of penance, with which she was
well supplied. There were a great many persons who, hearing by report of the rigid austerities of Mary Ann, became very urgent in
their entreaties to be admitted for a moment
into her quarters, to behold with their own eyes
what they had heard, to their great surprise,
about her: but it was not possible, when she
discovered their object, to induce her to satisfy
their curiosity. Once, however, she could not
escape, without disobeying the many pressing
solicitations made her by D. Giuseppa Tinco, a
lady belonging to one of the first families and
of great piety. This lady, after having begged
of the servant of God with a great deal of
earnestness but always in vain, to be allowed to
see her rooms, had at last recourse to her confessor, and obtained from him a positive order.
Then Mary Ann finding it imposible to offer
further resistance, fled to prayer to consult her
Divine Spouse; and she arose from it so consoled, that D. Scolastica Sarmiento, who had
brought her the command of her confessor, she
said—"You will see that Signora Tinco, although she has got the permission of my con-

fessor, will not gain her object;" and she added,
"I have asked of my Spouse not to cause me
the pain I would experience were that lady permitted to enter my poor chamber, because she
would see things there which I would not wish
any one to see." And so in fact it happened;
for the lady, after being kindly led into the first
room of the apartment, no sooner cast her eye
upon the coffin that was in the middle of the
floor, with the skeleton in it, than she was
seized with such horror that she fainted on the
spot, and not wishing to advance any farther, it
was necessary to raise her up and carry her insensible out of the apartment.

Even Catharine, the Indian servant, and D.
Sebastiana her niece, who dwelt in the same
apartment, could very seldom gain admittance
into the more private rooms of Mary Ann,
where she kept her instruments of penance.
The blessed girl was there all alone, either
absorbed in deep contemplation, or mortifying
her innocent body in the most unheard-of ways:
and she never left them, except it was at noon
to serve at the table of her relatives, or towards
evening to recite with them the holy rosary, or
to read some pious book. The rest of the day

she was never seen wandering through the other parts of the house, or stopping to entertain herself with any one, although it were only for a moment.

She never left the house when she was in good health, except to go every morning to the church of the Society of Jesus, where she spent her time praying and solacing herself with the holy Sacraments till it was eleven o'clock. She always went and returned by the shortest and most expeditious way; and such was her modesty and composure that the very sight of her was calculated to excite one to devotion. She wore a long veil which reached to her breast, and with it she completely covered her face and hands; and she walked with such recollection, that she noticed none who passed her, and it frequently became necessary for her nieces and the other ladies who accompanied her to warn her to return the salutations of many persons who came purposely at that hour to meet and recommend themselves to her. From the testimony in the different processes, we learn that she only went once to the church of St. Francis to assist, as we said before, at the obsequies of her niece D. Sebastiana; and on another occa-

sion she once changed her ordinary way to the
church of the Jesuits. The cause of it was this:
When she was either going or returning from
the church, some persons seeing her at a distance, made use of these words: "Look, here
comes the Saint;" and this was the common
name by which she was called by every body in
Quito. Mary Ann heard the words, and it cannot be imagined how painful they were to her
humility. She shed copious tears before her
God, and for many days increased her ordinary
mortifications. She deprived herself of that
trifling refreshment which she took to quench
her burning thirst, by keeping in her mouth
small pieces of apple and extracting the juice;
and she tortured herself with other penances, as
if she would punish in herself the esteem and
good opinion which others had of her. And
finally, she proposed, in her own mind, to alter
her rout, and in fact she did so the next morning to escape hearing similar expressions of esteem. But having confided the whole affair, as
was her custom, to her confessor, he thought
otherwise, and she immediately submitted her
will to his. When she was invited by her nieces
and her other female relatives to go with them

to some extraordinary and solemn sacred function, that was celebrated in the city, she always
excused herself by saying, that she could not
do so without special leave of her confessor
Suppressing in this manner every emotion of
curiosity, although perfectly innocent, she persevered to her death, spending her days entirely
hidden in her own rooms, or in the church of
the Jesuits.

All this arose from the little value Mary Ann
set on the things of this world.   Accustomed
from her tender years to know and contemplate
with the eyes of the mind the incomparable
greatness of heaven, every time she cast her eye
upon the goods here below, she could never discover in them any thing to be derived as precious, but rather why they should be abhorred
as vile and sordid.   From this same source also
sprung the small account she made of beauty of
person, nobility of blood, abundance of riches,
and whatever the world loves and embraces,
and holds as the chief happiness of man.   From
the time she consecrated herself to God by a
perpetual vow of poverty, she retained nothing
as her own, but as lent her by her sister D.
Girolama.   She lived in the house just as if she

had been taken in through charity, and maintained out of pure charity; the furniture of her rooms could not have been worse, or of a poorer description. The whole of it consisted of a painting of the most Blessed Trinity, two little statues of the Infant Jesus and his most Blessed Mother, and a few other simple pictures of her patron Saints. In addition to these she had a small bed and a few chairs, which were merely for show, a guitar on which she sometimes sang some pious hymns, some lives of the Saints and other spiritual books, a large collection of penetential instruments, and nothing more. It was her invariable custom to have no other dress than that she had on, which was, as we said, of plain serge, and which she mended with her own hand. She never made a present of the most trifling little thing without first getting the express consent of her confessor, neither did she ever take any thing of the house, even for her own use, without asking permission of her relatives. Whenever presents were offered or sent her by her friends, she either would not receive them, or if she were obliged for fear of giving offence to take them, she immediately distributed them to the poor. And with the

consent of her confessor she gave in the same
manner what she gained by the labour of her
hands during the hours which were not devoted
to the concerns of her soul.

But the perfect detachment from the goods
of the earth, and the voluntary renunciation
made of them by means of evangelical poverty,
however hard it may be to the flesh, which is
constrained to subject itself to continual incon-
venience and trouble, bears no comparison with
the excellence of that virtue which is necessary
for the bridling and correcting the interiour
passions of the soul, and to renounce one's own
will and judgment, following reason alone as a
guide, and the direction of those whom God has
given us to be our directors and masters. To
show how much the Blessed Mary Ann of Jesus
signalized herself in this regard, I could here
relate, if it would not take too long, the depositions of those who, of their own knowledge,
declared that she had arrived to a perfect mastery over the emotions of the soul in every kind
of affection. At the beginning of her devout
life, when that storm of contradictions, of which
we have already spoken, was raised against her,
even by persons of known probity and learning,

she was never observed to show any resentment,
or be in the least ruffled, but always the same,
she bore with a calm mind and serene look, and
with unalterable peace, the taunts and cutting
observations of her enemies. And as she had
been in the habit of conquering herself, she
succeeded in acquiring those two difficult things,
which constitute the perfection of virtue, viz:
to rejoice in scorn and contempt, as if they were
so many praises and honours, and to have such
an absolute mastery over herself as to render
her exempt from the violence of those first and
sudden emotions which frequently surprise and
overpower reason. Thus did this blessed soul
enjoy, as in a secure port, perpetual calm and
tranquillity; and whatever turn things took, far
from giving her any disturbance, they afforded
her, on the contrary, incomparable content and
delight, because in them she beheld the eternal
ordinations of divine providence. As far as she
was personally concerned, being fully persuaded
that the way of sufferings is the shortest and
the most profitable, she besought her beloved
Spouse continually, that should it please his
divine majesty that he would deign conduct her
to sanctity not by the extraordinary graces of

predilection, of which she thought herself unworthy, but by trials of humiliations, contempt,
and a life entirely hidden from the eyes of men.

It is not wonderful if to the interiour mortification of the affections of the soul, she added
a perfect renunciation of her own will and judgment. From the time she bound herself by the
vow of obedience to her confessor, we can say
with truth, she had no longer any will or judgment of her own, giving herself up entirely to
the guidance and direction of him who had
charge of her soul. Her first confessor was, as
we very frequently said, Father John Camaccio,
who undertook the direction of her from her
tender years, and under whose paternal care she
reached the highest point of perfection. After
him she had Fathers Antonio Monosalvas, Luigi
Vasquez, Luca della Queva, Gion Pietro Severino, Alfonso Roxas, and towards the last years
of her life, God himself, by a special disposition
of divine providence, gave her for her spiritual
director Brother Ferdinando della Croce, all of
them religious of the Society of Jesus. To them
she gave an exact account of her conscience
every day, and with much humility and wonderful sincerity manifested the interiour emotions

of her soul, the mortifications and penances
which she practised, and the favours which she
received from God: nor did she ever depart an
iota from their prescriptions, although they were
contrary and repugnant to her own views. Even
those very things which, of their nature, are extremely dear to a soul enamoured with God,
such as to go to church, to pray and receive the
Sacraments were only pleasing to her inasmuch
as they were done through obedience; and she
would have had a great scruple if she had suffered herself to be influenced by her fervour to
undertake any thing, however holy and good it
might be, from any other motive than to please
God and do his divine will, of which her confessors were the secure and legitimate interpreters.   At first, to put her virtue to the test,
sometimes one and sometimes another ordered
her not to approach the holy table; nay, more,
not to go to church: and she in the true spirit
of obedience resigned herself entirely to their
good pleasure.   The family were astonished to
see her stay at home on certain days and not
even hear mass; but no one, from respect to her,
dared to ask her the reason.   Only Catharine
the Indian, whom we have so frequently men-

tioned in this history, with impertinent simplicity asked her mistress, one morning, why
she was not getting ready that day to go to the
church, according to custom. And Mary Ann
told her, without being in the least disturbed,
"I am not going because I am a daughter of
obedience."

No matter how hard or difficult the things
were that were enjoined her, she never suffered
herself to be actuated by any judgment or sentiment contrary to the perfection of obedience.
To make a practical trial to what degree of subjection she had brought her will, Father Camaccio ordered her to lay open her whole interiour to her niece D. Giovanna di Casso, and
not conceal one thing either of her penances or
the divine favours which, up to that hour, she
had received in such abundance from the liberal
hand of the Lord; and at the same time he acquainted D. Giovanna with the order he had
given Mary Ann. Every one can imagine how
much it must have cost the servant of God
blindly to submit to such a command, overcoming with heroic fortitude every feeling of natural
repugnance, which was doubly increased from
the low opinion she had of herself. The fact

14

was, she was no sooner returned home than she
called aside her niece, and after telling her the
command she had received from her confessor,
with no less humility than sincerity, began to
manifest all the severe treatment which she had
ever inflicted on herself by the practice of so
many mortifications and penances; after this she
disclosed to her, one by one, the favours and
singular gifts which Almighty God had poured
into her bosom with such abundance and predilection; and she narrated every thing with as
much minuteness and sincerity as if she were
rendering an account to her confessor under
seal of confession. D. Giovanna was almost
beside herself through wonder; and this not so
much on account of that heroic act of obedience,
on the part of her aunt, as on account of the
great and extraordinary things which she heard.
She tried to impress them deeply upon her mind,
and scarcely was the other finished before she
arose to retire to her own room and put on
paper what she had heard. After going a few
steps she wished to call to mind what she had
heard, but she had only a general and confused
recollection. She remembered in general to
have heard things truly wonderful and extra-

ordinary; but in particular she remembered
nothing, her mind being filled with a thousand
strange and vague ideas. Wherefore being
more than ever astonished and perplexed at the
strangeness of the thing, she returned back into
the Saint's room and said—"Pray, tell me again,
I entreat you, what you just now told me; for
I don't know how, but I can't remember a single
word of all that you told me: you will not refuse
me this favour which I ask of you, since you
were already pleased to unbosom your whole
soul to me." But the servant of God, who was
perfectly aware of what had happened by a light
from above, smiled a little hearing her talk in
this manner; and notwithstanding the earnest
and humble entreaties which were made her,
she could never be induced to repeat a single
word, thinking it sufficient that she had punc-
tually executed the obedience imposed upon her.
Her niece, however, was not disheartened, but
renewing her entreaties she asked her "how will
I ever be able to reply to Father Camaccio,
should he wish to know of me if you have
obeyed?" Mary Ann, with the greatest mild-
ness, replied—"You will tell my father confessor that I have obeyed his command, but that

my heavenly Spouse does not wish my affairs to
be known whilst I am still alive: and this is
sufficient. For yourself, complain of your defi-
ciency of memory, and hence learn that it is the
will of God that his secrets should not be inves-
tigated." Nor did the wonder cease here; for,
after the death of Mary Ann, all the impressions
so long lost suddenly revived in the mind of
her niece clear and distinct; and so she was able
to recount a great portion of what, on that occasion, she had heard from her holy aunt.

Father Antonio Monosalvas confessed, in his
juridical deposition, that being still quite young
and not much skilled in the direction of souls
of consummate perfection and sanctity, it not
unfrequently happened that he commanded the
servant of God several things which were not
at all suited to that way of virtue, by which
God wished to direct her. Notwithstanding
this Mary Ann, although she plainly saw by a
light from above that her confessor was mistaken, obeyed to the very letter without reply.
Only the next day, when presenting herself before him, she humbly prayed him that " he would
be pleased to read, at his convenience, a particular chapter or paragraph which she had marked
in the book she gave him." And the Father

added, that "precisely in that very place he found the solution of his doubts, and discovering the mistake he had made, applied himself more and more earnestly to prayer, and implored light from heaven to enable him to conduct souls by that way, by which God called them to himself.

But where the humility and obedience of Mary Ann were displayed in their highest perfection was in the following fact. Since Brother Ferdinando della Croce, from that sympathetic feeling of the soul which existed between them, had a perfect knowledge of the marvellous life of that blessed soul, he thought with himself that it would greatly tend to God's glory, if she should undertake, through obedience, to write an exact account of her whole life, and by this means the world would have from herself an exact detail of her virtues, and those most singular favours which God had bestowed upon her. He commanded her, therefore, under pain of disobedience, to write down a faithful narrative of every thing that had passed up to that moment in her innocent soul. Any one who knows any thing of perfection may easily judge what an heroic act is required to obey such a command, especially in the case of an humble and holy person. Mary Ann was touched to the very quick; and as she knew that it was not contrary to the perfection of the will prompt to obey, to propose with due deference to her superiour her reasons to the contrary, she signified to her director what her humility and contempt of herself suggested, in order to rid herself of the task imposed upon her, if they should seem good to him. But the good religious, after having listened with attention to all her reasons, concluded by telling her bluntly and in few words, that she must obey. She submissively bowed her head, and suppressing every natural repugnance, immediately began to execute the order that had been given her. And she had already accomplished a good portion of her task, when learning by a light from above that such was not the will of her Divine Spouse, she returned to Brother Ferdinando and briefly informed him of the interiour voice she had heard, but with entire resignation to his judgment. He seeing that it was the will of God, yielded and revoked his order; and she immediately tearing in pieces what she had written joyfully gave up the undertaking, and thus we were deprived of that most interesting account of her interiour life.

CHAPTER X.

THE GREAT LOVE OF THE BLESSED MARY ANN
TOWARDS GOD. HER ARDENT DESIRE TO SUFFER,
AND THE INCREDIBLE DELIGHT SHE EXPERIENCED
IN SUFFERINGS.   HER INNOCENCE OF LIFE AND
THE ANGELIC PURITY OF HER MANNERS, WHICH
SHE PRESERVED UNSPOTTED TO HER DEATH.—
WONDERFUL EFFECTS OF THE SAME.

THE more the Blessed Mary Ann was free
from the empire of the passions and detatched
from the love of creatures, the more she was
intimately connected with and united to God.
All her thoughts and affections were turned to
her chief good; and from the divine love they
derived their origin, regulation and direction,
and in the divine love terminated her every
action It is only from the effects which it produced that we can form any idea of the ardent
love which burnt continually in her heart: and
these effects could not have been clearer or of a
more wonderful character. Among these were
the gift of tears, the visible fire that appeared

in her countenance, the power of remaining
hours and whole nights motionless and in a state
of ecstacy, encircled by rays, and transported
out of her senses, and sometimes also raised with
her whole body above the ground. In the church
of the Jesuits her ordinary place was under the
steps which led to the pulpit; and she chose this
in preference, both from humility and in order
to be less observed. But she did not gain her
end; for those present perceiving the frequent
and wonderful raptures of her soul in God—
even ladies of the highest nobility strove with
each other to place themselves at her side, and
to feel devotion at the very sight of her. Having gone early one morning to church with the
other ladies, her relatives, she remained the
whole morning upon her knees, as motionless as
if she had been a statue, and buried in profound
contemplation. The hour was already late and
near noon, and consequently the ladies, wishing
to return home, went up to Mary Ann and
saluted her. She did not perceive them although
they called her several times, and shook her by
her clothes and by her arm. Then D. Maria de
Paredes raised her veil, which reached almost
to her very feet, and with her companions saw

her in ecstacy, transported out of herself, with
her hands crossed upon her breast, her mouth
wide open, and a smile playing upon her lips,
and her eyes filled with tears and fixed on heaven. They would not disturb her, but went
home, leaving her to enjoy the delights of paradise.

She felt such a spiritual relish in conversing
of God, that she seemed to have had him always
present, as she was always united to him in
mind and heart. She was asked one day by D.
Petronilla of St. Bruno, her great friend, to play
her a tune on a kind of lute, and she consented.
But after a few moments she suddenly stopped
still, with her hands resting on the strings, and
became, as it were, ecstatic for the space of an
entire hour: at length, coming to herself and
with her face all inflamed, "Oh, Petronilla," she
exclaimed, "what great things there are in
paradise!" She could say this much and no more,
when she was interrupted by the vehemence of
her affection and a copious shower of tears. In
her solitude also she kept, as we said before, a
musical instrument, and with it she was wont to
raise her heart to God, accompanying the music
with her voice. But it happened very, often

that after a few moments she was obliged to cease altogether, being overcome by the interiour emotions of her affections. She had composed for her own use some stanzas in rhyme, and they were burning aspirations of her love towards God. Hence we are not to be surprised that some of the witnesses testified that they frequently heard in her rooms a chorus of the sweetest voices; and since there is no doubt that she was alone, their suspicion was not improbable that the angels united their voices with hers to praise together their common Creator.

Every thing which came under her eyes served as an occasion to her to raise her heart to God, therefore she was often seen all inflamed with the divine love, fainting and languishing like a pure lily before the scorching beams of the sun. The plants, the flowers, the herbs, the waters, all creatures were so many voices to her, which made her heart throb with joy. I will say, moreover, that in the evils and miseries of this world she found a motive to love God more and more. Conversing one day with D. Eleonora Rodriguez, they began to speak together of the calamities and dangers which are encountered in this mortal life: in which conversation the

servant of God became very much excited, and
turning to that pious lady, she told her that
when she considered the miseries of this life
and the dangers which are found in it, she became inflamed as a burning coal, and fled for
refuge to the side of Jesus Christ, and there
took up her repose.

But the most convincing proof which we have
of her great love of God was undoubtedly the
great desire she had of suffering, and of suffering much, and of suffering more and more every
day. There were two causes which aroused
within her heart these generous desires, viz: to
become conformable to the image of Jesus
Christ, and the hope that her sufferings would
shorten her days, and unite her eternally to her
God. In her prayers, and especially on Fridays,
she was accustomed to ask of our Lord that he
would give her much to suffer, and the power
of exhibiting to Him some correspondence of
love. When she was afterwards attacked by
those long and painful infirmities, her ordinary
relief was to repeat with unalterable peace,
" May it be all for the love of God." At other
times she was in the habit of saying, with great
affection—"Oh, if one could enjoy God! oh, if

one could die for love of Him! oh, if one could
die to enjoy Him!" Speaking one day with
Petronilla of St. Bruno, she candidly confessed
that she felt herself burning and consuming interiourly with the fire of the divine love. Then
like one in an ecstacy she went on repeating:
"Do you know, O, sister, that one of my feet is
already swelling, but it gives me no pain; for
the desire which I have of enjoying my God is
so great that death alone will satisfy me; I desire nothing but to die soon. St. Gertrude, my
patroness and mother, was pleased to visit me,
and after consoling me with her words has told
me that my Spouse has prepared for me seven
precious rings. Oh, that one could die for love
of Him! oh, that one could be entirely consumed with his love! oh, could one die in order
to enjoy Him forever!" Having said this, without another word, she suddenly left the company and withdrew to her rooms.

Not content with the horrible tortures which
she voluntarily inflicted on her body, she had
a holy envy for those martyrs who had suffered
more in hatred of the faith for the love of Jesus
Christ. Having heard, one evening, the passion
of a holy martyr read, she became so inflamed

that she prayed our Lord to make her suffer
some extraordinary torment.   Having therefore
gone to bed, after a short sleep she awoke with
her whole body racked with terrible pains, one
foot being contracted, an arm palsied, her tongue
parched and wounded, and her whole person so
bruised and sore as to be unable to move without the assistance of others.   Her relatives
hastened to her and anxiously inquired the cause
of so great an affliction.   She dissembled a little,
but when she saw that they were going to send
immediately for the physicians, she told them,
with a great deal of simplicity, that they should
not trouble themselves about her sufferings:
that they were the delights of her heavenly
Spouse, sent her to satisfy, in some manner, the
ardent love she had of suffering for the faith.
And she related that it seemed to her in her
sleep that she had been actually in the islands
of Japan, where those barbarians had tormented
her with no ordinary cruelty.   It was precisely
at this time that the persecutions against the
Japanese Christians were raging with the greatest violence: and Mary Ann, reading the ac-
counts which came thence, was inflamed every
day more and more with the desire of partaking

15

also in the like torments, and it was sometimes miraculously granted her by Almighty God. She even once hinted to one of her more confidential friends, that the acute pains which she was then suffering corresponded exactly to the torments inflicted on the martyrs in Japan. And she continued no less than three months in this state of painful martyrdom.

Father Luca della Cueva related in his deposition that, having gone to visit Mary Ann, who was lying sick in bed, and having been greatly edified to see that in place of complaining of her painful malady, she burnt with a desire of suffering still more, he recited to her that passage of Job, (ch. vi. 8,) *Who will grant that my request may come, and that he that hath begun may destroy me; and that this may be my comfort, that afflicting me with sorrow he spare not?* which was precisely in accordance with the spirit of the servant of God. That after having briefly expounded and commented upon it, he told her of what had happened in Toledo, in Spain, to a very virtuous young lady, and a penitent of Father Baldassarre Alvarez, that great spiritual master. This lady had been sent, without any fault of hers, into the prisons of the holy Inquisition, and remained there without justifying herself, as she could easily have done. But Father Alvarez taking up her defence, she obtained her liberty. At which the fervorous young lady was not only not pleased, but going to Father Alvarez expostulated with him saying: "Ah, Father, my Father! how I regret that I lost the chance of receiving two hundred lashes in the public streets of Toledo?" Wishing to signify by this that she, without any fault on her side, would gladly have submitted to any ill treatment for the love of God. When he had finished his narration, Father della Cueva asked Mary Ann "If she were also ready to be beaten through the streets of Quito?" And she immediately replied, "I am ready, perfectly ready;" and she added, moreover, that "she said it with all her heart." The words of the Father remained afterwards so deeply engraven upon her mind, that being obliged a few days later to start for his missions among the heathens, after several months he received a letter from Mary Ann, in which she entreated him to send her in writing that sentence of Job, in order that she might have it continually before her eyes and meditate upon it. In fine, to be brief, the love she had for suffering was insatiable, and she seemed to know of no other happiness than humiliations, infirmities, pains, which were dearer and more precious, just as they were more sensible and painful, glorifying God in them, for whose love she rejoiced in sufferings.

We must now speak of the two principal effects of her love towards God, which are the care she had of never offending him in the least, and of always keeping her soul united to him by means of prayer. As to Mary Ann's great purity of conscience I shall be very brief, giving only the testimony of her confessors, all of whom affirmed with one voice that for the space of twenty-six years that she lived, she never stained her baptismal innocence, not only by no serious sin, but not even by the smallest deliberate venial transgression. Every morning, before going to communion, she presented herself at the tribunal of penance, and there shed an abundance of bitter tears of repentance, as if she had been the greatest sinner in the world. And yet she never had any thing of which to accuse herself, except some trifling levities and inadvertencies committed in the first years of her life, before

she had attained the full use of reason. Besides
the two general and particular examens which
she made every morning and evening, at every
hour of the day she recollected herself, and carefully scrutinized her every action to see, I will
not say if she had committed any defect, but
whether she had performed them in the best,
most perfect and pleasing manner to God.

Hence we must not be surprised if she observed, with the greatest exactness and perfection to her death, the vow of virginal chastity,
by which she bound herself to God forever, before she had attained her eighth year. The
purity of her soul and body was always extreme;
and her confessors themselves knew not what
other name to give it than by saying that it was
altogether *wonderful, rare, singular, extraordinary, angelical.* Father Camaccio attested that
Mary Ann *had made a vow of purity and virginity, which she preserved unstained by the
least thought or imagination which could cast a
shadow or blemish upon it.* And Father Monosalvas affirmed, under oath, that *her chastity
was angelical, and that she never accused herself
of any thing that was at all contrary to holy
purity; and she was accustomed to give God*

15*

thanks that she did not even know what it was.
And Father Roxas added, *that according to her
belief, things contrary to purity never entered
the minds of virgins.* By a singular favour of
heaven, therefore, Mary Ann had the extremely
rare privilege of being entirely free and exempt
from every interiour combat, and from the least
rebellion of the flesh.

The fact is, it was sufficient for any one to
become enamoured with purity merely to look
at her; her face reflected the interiour beauty
and innocence of her soul: and she was so extremely jealous of it that she observed the
strictest watch to preserve it from every breath
that could tarnish it. Both in going to the
church as well as in returning, her carriage was
slow, extremely modest, with her face covered
and her eyes fixed upon the ground: and when
she was stopped by any one desirous of speaking
to her, she disengaged herself in few and well-
measured words as soon as she could. She never
admitted a male person into her rooms; and
once, when Maria de Paredes, her relative, informed her that a man was at the door who
desired to consult her about some doubts of his
soul, between wonder and horror she exclaimed.

"And what is this? A man wants to speak with me? I pray you that you bring no man to speak with me, and if he will return again you will say to him that I have no permission of my confessor to speak with him, and if he come to confer with me on any business of importance, let him go and consult the Fathers of the Society."

It will be seen still better by the following incident, how extremely delicate she was in this regard. A member of the Royal Audience of Quito, a man well advanced in years, distinguished for his good sense, and a man of eminent piety, on account of the great and wonderful things he had heard of her, had conceived the highest opinion of Mary Ann's sanctity, and desired, the first opportunity he should have, to see her and become personally acquainted with her. He happened to meet her one day in the public street, when she was on her way home from the church of the Jesuits, and being struck with her angelic modesty and the profound recollection of her carriage, he stopped to behold her, and when she was sufficiently near, he presented himself before her, humbly asking her that she would recommend him to God; after this he extended his hands, and in token of

reverence and respect embraced her. At this
unexpected occurrence the chaste virgin blushed
deeply, and without saying a word, as if beside
herself for shame, fled quickly home, where she
had hardly arrived before she burst into a flood
of tears, as if she had committed some great
fault or crime. After having given vent to her
grief for some time, she related, still weeping
to D. Sebastiana her niece, what had happened
to her; and when the other, after hearing the
cause, began to console him, saying, that " she
had no reason to afflict herself, since there was
no malice in the act, and she was not at all ac-
cessory to it;" "yes," replied the servant of
God, " all this I know and believe, and in truth
it is as you say: nevertheless, what will my
Divine Spouse say, who is jealous of my honour?"
She allowed herself no peace, till it seemed to
her that she had cancelled by her many and
severe penances every shade of sin that might
have been contracted by her.

Up to the last moments of her life there was
nothing which she recommended with greater
earnestness, and left it besides in writing, than
that as soon as she was dead, her sister D. Girolama, and her niece D. Giovanna, with another

lady, her confidant, should dress her body with the greatest decency, and should not allow any other ladies to approach to touch it. For the same reason she begged of Almighty God, with many prayers, that her body should not be preserved uncorrupt after her death; because she did not like, as she told her confessor, to be seen and handled by any one although a corpse. And in fact we shall see, in its proper place, that she miraculously gave signs of the repugnance she felt in this regard even upon her bier, when some person approached to kiss her in token of respect.

The virginal modesty and purity of Mary Ann were so well known and public all over the city of Quito, that no one ever dared to use language towards her that could be in the least offensive, except a certain individual who was a perfect stranger to her. Whilst she was one day in the church, perfectly recollected, and with her heart and mind fixed on God, an impertinent young man coming in by accident, approached her and with bold effrontery requested her to uncover her face. For some time Mary Ann paid no attention to the fellow's insolent demand; but when he became bolder, and insisted

on it for the third time, the modest young lady,
as if inspired by Almighty God, raised her veil
a little which concealed her head and face, and
in a firm and resolute voice said to him—" What
do you wish, sir?   I am here learning how to
die, you sir, do the same, if you wish to save
your soul."   And having said this she turned
to wrap herself up as before in her cloak.
Whether it were the tone of voice, or really, as
some of the witnesses deposed, he saw in place
of Mary Ann's face, by a miracle, nothing less
than a horrible skull, the impudent fellow seeing
her turn and speak to him in that manner, was
completely abashed, and trembling from head to
foot, ran and fled into the sacristy of the same
church, where, trembling from head to foot, he
related to those he found there what had occurred, who, instead of compassionating him,
rebuked him severely, calling him a devil for
daring to tempt that angel of modesty and innocence.

It is true, that after this the spirit of darkness was the only external enemy who endeavoured to disturb the peace of Mary Ann, and
Almighty God permitted it as a greater trial of
her virtue.   A great number therefore of devils,

taking visible forms, presented themselves frequently before this innocent virgin in horrid
and lewd shapes. When she saw these disgusting images before her she was filled with a holy
horror, and shutting her eyes raised her mind
and heart to God, entreating him to come to her
aid and rescue: and this alone was sufficient to
put the whole host of these malicious spirits
immediately to flight. Failing in this attempt,
the infernal enemy tried a more cunning artifice.
One day, when Mary Ann was in church, a very
handsome and polite young man accosted her,
who, presenting himself to her in a very fascin-
ating manner, offered his services, giving every
evidence of his admiration of her. By a supernatural light the chaste virgin saw at first sight
through the treacherous mask which the devil
had assumed to deceive her; therefore, without
more, with an air of scorn and cutting sarcasm,
she told him, that he should make these offers
of service and regard to God his Creator, and
ask pardon of him for his intolerable pride. As
for herself, being a poor miserable sinner, she
was in no way worthy of being esteemed or
honoured by any one. The proud spirit could
not stand these words, and disappeared in an ir.

stant, nor did he ever afterwards molest the
servant of God on this point.

Finally, I am persuaded that that most delicious odour which the body of Mary Ann ex-
haled, and which communicated itself to every
thing which she used, was the effect or demonstration of her immaculate purity. Such at least
was the unanimous opinion of all the witnesses
who gave evidence in the different processes.
They said that both her person as well as her
clothes, sent forth almost always such a fragrant
odour, that had they not known her abhorrence
for every kind of delicacy, they would have
been convinced that she made use of the most
precious perfumes. And Catharine the Indian
affirmed, that when she entered her rooms, she
perceived an odour which might be called heavenly. The blood taken from her veins, besides
preserving its purity, emitted an agreeable
odour: a most beautiful lily sprung from it, as
we shall relate more at large in its proper place.
The same odour of lilies was perceived many
years after her death, not once, but many times,
in the apartment formerly inhabited by her
And finally, it can be said, that the miracle still
continues down to our own day, since her bones,

although left for a long time in unslacked lime, preserve still at the present moment—even the smallest fragments, an aromatic and most agreeable odour, as every one may judge for himself. But what we have briefly said, will suffice for the present, as we intend to speak of it more in detail in another place.

CHAPTER XI.

THE HIGH DEGREE OF PRAYER TO WHICH THE BLESSED MARY ANN WAS RAISED BY ALMIGHTY GOD. THE CONTINUAL BUT VAIN ASSAULTS OF THE DEVIL TO DIVERT HER FROM IT. THE HEROIC RESIGNATION AND PATIENCE SHE DISPLAYED IN TIME OF ARIDITY AND DESOLATION OF SPIRIT. GOD PROVIDES HER WITH AN EXPERIENCED DIRECTOR WHO CONSOLES HER.

LET us now come to prayer, which is, as we said above, another effect of consummate charity. How the Blessed Mary Ann of Jesus advanced in this holy exercise, from grade to grade, her very infancy gives evidence, as the Holy Ghost himself, without the aid of human instruction,

taught her to withdraw herself from the most
familiar friends and hide herself in the woods,
or in some secluded part of the house, and there
remain in prayer with such interiour satisfaction
that hours passed away as if they were moments,
and she became insensible to every thing exteriour. As she advanced in years, and by the
continual practice of meditating, she reached
that best and most perfect degree, which is to
keep the mind always fixed on God, and absorbed in the highest contemplation. Father
Camaccio affirmed this of her in these express
words—"Our Lord raised her to the highest
degree of contemplation, which consists in knowing God and his perfections without reasoning,
and of loving him without interruption." And
the same thing all her other confessors confirmed, adding that "she never lost sight of her
God, having him always present by the most
intimate communication of spirit, and that to
have material for contemplation, she had no
farther need of books or any other thing, since
all that she saw or heard served as a ladder to
mount to God and repose in him, loving him
with her whole heart."

The time which she expressly allotted to it

always consisted of many hours of the day and
of the night; for it can be truly said that her
whole life was one prolonged meditation and
prayer. And this was observed by those of her
own household, who almost always found her on
her knees immovable, and praying with such
intensity that it was not sufficient to call her
several times, or shake her very forcibly in
order to make her recover her senses. Neither
was she herself, although anxious to avoid any
exteriour demonstration, such a mistress of her
own actions, inasmuch as she could not, when
she wished, recall her mind from this continual
abstraction. What were the special illumina-
tions, the extraordinary lights, the favours, the
delights and the heavenly sweetnesses which
she imbibed from prayer with those other en-
joyments which Almighty God communicated
to her soul in his conversation with her, are
only really known and appreciated by those who
have experinced them. We can only say that
great indeed must have been the advantages
and fruit which she derived from that familiar
communication with her Beloved, since the
devil employed every means to disturb her in
this holy exercise.

Sometimes there issued from under the little
altar, before which Mary Ann prayed in her
room, a great quantity of egg-shells which, being
put in motion without any visible cause, struck
against each other and made a considerable
noise; at other times a small knife was seen to
move, as if in the hand of some unseen person,
which would approach her neck and seem about
to strike it. But the servant of God very soon
discovering the pitiful artifice of the tempter,
would not even deign to turn her head, or give
herself the least uneasiness. The enemy being
provoked at this, appeared to her in a visible
and more horrible form, threatening her with
a sword in his hand. But she told him, with
great peace and tranquillity, that "he was losing
his time, hoping in that manner to divert her
from her meditation; that she was a weak and
sinful creature, but had placed all her confidence in her heavenly Spouse, who would protect her." The devil being again overcome,
changed his manner, and began, under the appearance of a horrible mastiff, to bark and run
up and down the rooms. Mary Ann, for some
time, bore with this annoyance, but at last she
took the resolution to go up to him boldly and

catch him, and having secured him tied him to
the foot of the bed. This having, by some
means or other, come to the knowledge of one
of her nieces, she asked her "If she were not
afraid to catch the devil with her hands and tie
him in that manner?" And she replied, "Why
should I be afraid of that dog, which can do
nothing but bark?" She said no more, and immediately changed the conversation.

The evil one did not however merely confine
himself to threats and barking only, but several
times vented his rage against her by striking
her and maltreating her in every part of her
body, and especially her tongue, which, as some
of the family deposed, was seen one morning
hanging from her lips, suspended only by a thin
thread of skin. Mary Ann was not frightened
at this; but having replaced her lacerated
tongue in her mouth with her own hands, and
collected her strength the best way she could,
she went to the church, communicated, and returned home perfectly cured. I will add, in
conclusion to this subject, the relation of a singular adventure, in which it would be difficult
to say, whether the constancy or generosity of
mind of our saint were more conspicuously dis-

played. One night, whilst she was buried in a profound meditation, she perceived that the light, which she always kept burning in her apartment, was suddenly extinguished: and knowing well that this was one of the usual insults offered her by the devil, without caring about relighting the lamp, she approached the coffin in the dark, and, taking out the skeleton, stretched herself in its place in order to continue her prayer in peace. The next morning, at day-break, she rose from the coffin and deliberately opened the window-shutter in order to give light to the room. Here a spectacle met her eyes which she had not expected. The skeleton was no longer lying upon the floor, where she had placed it, but was standing erect upon its feet, and leaning against the wall, with its dry hands crossed upon its breast, and wearing a most dreadful and terrible look. Mary Ann did not faint away at the sight, because she was supported in a special manner by Almighty God, but she could not but feel a lively and natural horror. For a moment she stood motionless and irresolute: then a ray of light penetrating her mind, she knew that this must be a new trick of the enemy to frighten her, sprin-

kled the skeleton with holy water, and courageously taking it up in her arms immediately
turned to place it, as it was before, in the coffin.

But the longest and most painful battles which
Mary Ann had to encounter for her greater
merit did not come from hell but from heaven.
Some years had passed in an undisturbed peace
and security, when all at once she found herself
involved in the midst of the darkness of obscu-
rity and perplexity, with her heart oppressed
by aridity and desolation of spirit.   Losing all
taste and relish for the things of God, the very
attempt of applying herself to prayer or of reading any spiritual book was one and the same
thing as to feel herself oppressed with a deep
sadness and annoyance.   The trial was indeed
hard and difficult for a soul so enamoured with
God, and accustomed, from her tender years, to
be always united to him, and to revel in the
delights of paradise.   Father Camaccio, her confessor, went so far as to say that "the tedious-
ness, the desolation and the interiour anguish
which she suffered were such that they would
long before have deprived her of life had not
God, in his wisdom, miraculously preserved it in
order to increase her merit. In this multiplicity

of afflictions, far from despondency, she persevered with heroic constancy firm in the divine
love, observing exactly the distribution of time
prescribed for prayer, and seeking continually
in the midst of darkness her Beloved, who
seemed purposely to hide himself for the purpose of increasing her sufferings.

She had always in her prayer, as Father Camaccio informs us, earnestly begged of God that
he would conduct her by the way of tribulations
and not by that of heavenly delights: and hence
seeing herself now at last heard, it seemed that
she should have rejoiced at it.   But as God ordained, two grievous fears assailed her at the
very moment.   In regard to men she was afraid
lest she should appear to them troublesome and
annoying on account of her melancholy, or of
losing in speaking her usual affability and meek-
ness: and in respect to God she feared, lest she
had merited on account of her sins, that the
Lord should withdraw himself from her, and
therefore she regarded as the chastisement of a
guilty and ungrateful soul, that which the Lord
had permitted in his other servants to render
them stronger and more generous in his love.
In this manner, deprived of every interiour con-

solation, and besides this fearful of not being pleasing to her Spouse, the more faithfully she advanced in the love of God, and hence in perfection and virtue, so much the more she turned this love itself into a terrible martyrdom.

To crown the series of her troubles, she was unexpectedly deprived of Father John Camaccio her confessor, in whom she had placed all her confidence. God permitted that the Superiours of the Society, being at some variance of opinion with regard to the daily communions of Mary Ann, should judge it advisable to change his residence and send him to labour in another College far from Quito. By this unforseen accident the servant of God found herself in a double abyss of trouble and affliction, first because it seemed to her that she had been the cause of the Father's removal, and secondly because by his departure she had lost an experinced director who, having regulated her conscience from her tender years, could then, more than any one else, afford her assistance and comfort. Nevertheless, conquering herself by an act of pure virtue, she submitted with heroic resignation to the divine will, and was perfectly ready to continue without any solace to her

death in that state of affliction. Father Camaccio being gone, she took Father Monosalvas for
her confessor, who had already many times
directed her in her spiritual concerns; and she
was just beginning to breathe a little, when she
was also deprived of him, being called to a distant place to perform various services for the
glory of God. She finally selected Father Luigi
Vasquez, Rector of the University of Quito, a
wise and learned man, but not at all suited to
have the direction of her soul. He guided her
by a way not adapted to the interiour dispositions in which she actually was, nor applicable
to her present wants; and she suffered herself
to be directed by him, and obeyed him to the
very letter in every thing, although he was well
aware and saw by experience that the bitterness
of her spirit and her interiour desolations daily
increased. She shed burning tears, begging
light and assistance not to go astray in such a
state of uncertainty, and in the midst of such
palpable darkness; and at last God, moved to
pity at the afflictions of his faithful servant,
after so long an experiment, consoled her, making her hear one night, whilst she was in the
act of praying, these clear and distinct words:

"Go to the church of the Jesuits, as is your custom; and speak and open your whole interiour to the first religious, who will enter the church by the door of the chapel of St. Xavier. He will be your spiritual father and assist you."

It was hardly day before Mary Ann hastened to the church, and having placed herself upon her knees opposite the door of the Sacristy, which was contiguous to the chapel of St. Francis Xavier, saw a lay-brother, after a few minutes, enter the church by that door, a man of much simplicity and of great perfection, who was well known all over the city. By means of the Sacristan she requested to speak with him, but he excused himself, saying, that "he could not talk to her without the permission of his Superiour." This very reply confirmed her more and more that he must be the one whom God has destined to be her guide and master in the affairs of her soul : and therefore having immediately obtained the permission of the Superiour of the College, she unfolded to him standing, just as he was, in one corner of the church, her state, opening her whole soul to him. The good brother, upon hearing such extraordinary acts of virtue and perfection, was so much consoled

and out of himself, that returning to the Sacristy
he could not refrain from exclaiming in the
fervour of his joy—"Oh, how admirable is God
in his Saints! This young lady is nothing less
than another St. Catharine of Sienna; she is an
angel in flesh." And this is that brother Ferdinando della Croce, whom God, in the secrets
of his wisdom, has selected to be the director
of a soul so dear to and beloved by him. From
the very first interview they contracted that interiour communication of soul, which afterwards
continued to the death of Mary Ann. It seemed
at first to many a very strange thing, and not at
all according to the rules of human prudence;
but in the end all agreed in admiring the won-
derful.dispositions of Almighty God, who often-
times makes use of means in appearance the
weakest and most unfit to accomplish great
things, and selects the simple and the humble
of heart to confound the pride of the wise of
this world.

And as for Mary Ann, she was so consoled
from that first and brief conversation she had
with Ferdinando, that all her darkness was immediately dissipated, every anxiety banished,
and her former serenity of mind and peace of

heart again restored to her. But it will be
better to hear herself in her letter to Father
Monosalvas: "God," said she, "is a good con-
soler of the poor and the desolate. May he be
forever blessed: Amen. My Father, ever since
I advised with brother Ferdinando della Croce
about the affairs of my soul, I am leading a very
joyful life, and his words have afforded me much
consolation. The fact is, my Father, he is a
Saint. I only confess to Father Vasquez. God
has so ordained it: who can resist him? May
his will be done." And in another letter to the
same Father she adds—"I treat the concerns
of my soul with brother Ferdinando della Croce,
and he gives me much consolation. His only
desire is that I be a Saint, and that I be well
grounded in the virtue of humility, in order to
mount to the summit of perfection by the steps
of faith, hope and charity. It is a common saying, that he who treats with a wise man will
soon be wise: this brother is a Saint." Thus
she wrote with her own hand.

Then after having returned infinite thanks to
Almighty God for having at length deigned to
look down upon her with a favourable eye, she
gave a very minute account to Ferdinando of

17

every thing that had taken place, up to that
hour, in her soul; explaining to him all her exercises of piety, her penances, her method of
prayer and the favours she received from God.
She submitted to his approval her diary, or the
distribution of the hours and the actions of the
day; and in every thing she abandoned herself
to his guidance and direction, not wishing, if it
were possible, to move so much as a step without the consent of Brother Ferdinando. She
used, therefore, to ask permission for the smallest things, and she did not dare to follow her
own will in any thing. If afterwards the least
doubt occurred to her mind, when at home,
whether she ought to undertake or leave off any
thing. she never wished to use her own judgment, but wrote the matter briefly upon paper
and sent it to her director, and in the meantime
awaited his reply.

This minuteness in the exercise of virtue,
which, to the eyes of the prudent of the world,
who have no idea of perfection, will seem more
like littleness of mind, is so pleasing to God
that he sometimes rewards it with evident miracles. D. Maria Arias testified in the process
that, "being one evening in the apartment of

Mary Ann, and some doubt occurring to her mind how she should act in an affair of little consequence, the servant of God took a pen in her hand and wrote a note asking the advice of her director. The hour being late, D. Maria was anxious to find out who would carry that note to the College of the Jesuits; and she affirmed upon oath that, without having seen any person start from the house nor any one return to it, in a short time she found in the hands of Mary Ann the answer written by Brother Ferdinando della Croce, and which was read in her presence." And she added, that " out of the respect she entertained for the sanctity of the servant of God, she dared not question her how it had happened: but that she was fully persuaded that God wished by this miracle to authenticate the perfect subjection and dependence which she professed towards her di rectors."

CHAPTER XII.

THE LOVE AND DEVOTION OF THE BLESSED MARY ANN FOR THE MOST AUGUST TRINITY, FOR THE MYSTERIES OF THE LIFE OP CHRIST, FOR THE MOST HOLY VIRGIN AND HER PATRON SAINTS.

CERTAIN works of piety, which we call devotions, which assist to keep the mind elevated above material things, and the heart united to God, are also parts of prayer. And although to some they may seem to be things of little moment, still seeing them not only practiced but strongly recommended by the Saints, we ought to set a high value on them, at least with respect to the source from which they take their rise, which is wont to be charity and religion. Mary Ann had also hers, and she practiced them during the whole course of her life.

And in the first place, she always honoured, as we have signified in many places, with an especial veneration the most august mystery of the adorable Trinity. She was particularly devout to the three divine persons, and as if they were present to her corporeal eyes, paid them the most profound acts of adoration. Every day she recited on her knees and with her arms extended in the form of a cross, the Apostles' creed thirty times, enlivening her faith in the most holy Trinity, and thanking him for the immense benefits conferred upon men. In the solemn commemoration which the church makes every year of this mystery, she passed many hours in its contemplation; she adorned in the best manner she could her domestic little altar, and invited her relatives and nieces to enter her apartment, and there recite some devout prayers.

Being particularly devoted to all the mysteries which related to the life and passion of Jesus Christ, she had frequently in her mouth and often repeated the following ejaculatory prayer: "Blessed be the hour in which my Lord Jesus Christ took human flesh, was born, died, and rose again, ascended into heaven, and in which he instituted the most holy Sacrament of the Eucharist." For the solemnity of Christmas she prepared herself every year by a devout novena, accompanied with severe penances and mortifications: and she caused all the domestics to do the same in the best manner they could

As that holy night drew near, Mary Ann could
not contain her joy. She passed it before a
representation of the manger, either in singing
devout hymns in honour of the new-born babe,
which she accompanied with a stringed instrument, or in pouring forth the warmest and most
tender affections of her amorous heart. And
with good reason, for it is said that the divine
Infant sometimes favoured her with his presence
and allowed himself to be seen and tenderly
caressed by her. In proof of it I will here relate a fact which I find recorded in the process
of beatification.

Cosimo di Salazar, son of the niece of D.
Giovanna di Casso, when he was quite a young
child, once entered Mary Ann's apartment, and
beginning to run about the rooms with childish
liberty, chanced to espy his aunt, who was wholly
taken up with her eyes fixed upon a beautiful
little Infant, which she was holding in her arms.
The child at this sight immediately turned back
and ran to call his mother, that she might come
and see his aunt, who was caressing a little child.
D. Giovanna knew very well that the servant
of God was alone, and therefore having strong
suspicions of what was really the case, softly

entered Mary Ann's rooms, in order to examine
every thing very carefully, but unfortunately
she met Mary Ann coming out, who perhaps
from having overheard the words of the young
Cosimo, dreaded a discovery, and therefore was
very anxious to conceal the fact, who said to
her—"Why do you suffer little boys to enter
my rooms?" Her niece pretended not to have
understood her; and turning back she began to
question her son minutely about the thing, in
order to find out what child it was that he had
seen his aunt holding in her arms, and he with
wonderful simplicity and innocence pointing
with his little hand to a frame, in which the
most Blessed Virgin, with the child Jesus in
her arms, was painted, said to his mother that
"that was the very child whom his aunt was
pressing to her bosom:" thus from the mouth of
the innocent child, incapable of feigning or of
telling a lie, was discovered the great favour
conferred by Almighty God on his beloved
servant.

I shall say nothing of her vehement love towards the passion of the Redeemer, and the
most blessed Eucharist, having already written
enough upon these points in the course of this

history. From the former, in which she contemplated the excessive love of the Son of God, who carried his love so far as to give his body and blood for the salvation of men, she learnt how to return the love of one who had subjected himself for love of her to unheard of ignominies and torments; and from the other, in which is contained the fountain itself, and the author of life and grace, she imbibed strength and vigour for soul and body to advance and increase every day in perfection and a more intimate union with God.

In proportion to the love which she bore to the Son of God, was her devotion towards his most holy Mother. She imbibed it, we may say, with her milk, and increased in it, always giving new proofs of her affection. She recited every morning by herself, as we saw in her distribution of time, the holy Rosary; and in the evening she repeated it over again with the family. Every day also she recited the whole of the little office of the Virgin, divided into separate parts, and gave to each part the time and hour prescribed for it. For all the festivals of our Lady she prepared herself with extraordinary fervour, and increased her prayers and penances;

and on the festival itself she distributed to the poor, with the permission of her brother-in-law, more abundant alms. There was in the street, opposite to one of the windows of her apartment, a devout chapel dedicated to the most Blessed Virgin called of the angels, to which Mary Ann frequently turned, imploring her blessing from a distance, and to whom she paid her devotions. She sent every Saturday to this chapel two wax candles and several boquets of flowers; and in order not to be discovered, she made use of an Indian woman, who secretly carried this pious offering. She succeeded in keeping the thing a secret for some time: but at last, the sacristan being moved by the desire of finding out the person who regularly sent that present, one Saturday cautiously followed the Indian, and having seen her enter the house of Mary Ann, went in after her, and presenting himself before the servant of God, gave her a thousand thanks. But she, interrupting him in the middle of his discourse, "May God grant us," said she, "his grace and knowledge to serve his Blessed Mother; happy is the man who serves so great a Lady:" and having said this, she politely took her leave without wishing to hear anything further. In the church of the Jesuits she passed long hours before an altar of our Lady of Loretto; and she experienced such sensible delight that she seemed unable to tear herself away from it. She often spoke of Mary with such spiritual delight and tenderness of affection, that it was evident the mouth spoke from the abundance of the heart. My Queen, my Mistress, my Mother, Virgin of Virgins, and such like were the glorious titles dictated by her tender love towards the most holy Virgin; and when uttering them her whole face would become inflamed, her eyes sparkle, and her whole person so agitated, that she excited in every one who heard or saw her, fervorous sentiments of piety and devotion. Whatever graces she afterwards desired, she obtained them all by directing her supplications to this divine Mother. To every one also who professed himself her servant, she gave assurance that his petitions would be heard.

The proof of it, she said, she had experienced in her own case from childhood. Whilst she was still quite a young child, a disease settled on one of her fingures, which, besides causing her intolerable pain, threatened to terminate in a gangrene. D. Scolastica perceiving it, advised her to attend to it and call in the assistance of a surgeon. But the servant of God, with a joyful countenance, told her not to make herself uneasy about her, that there would be no need of so much trouble: after this, agitated by an interiour spirit which moved her, she rose and added :—"Wait a little, and you will see how I will cure it." Saying this, she knelt down before an image of the most Blessed Virgin, and full of confidence, asked her assistance in her present need; that was enough, for in an instant every sign of the ulcer disappeared, and her finger was perfectly cured. She herself was astonished at the quick and evident miracle, and warmly begged her friend to keep it secret.

Another time the humours that collected in her eyes caused her such a sharp and sensible pain that she was in great danger of going blind. Various remedies were applied to them; which, in place of giving any relief, tended only to increase the merit of her sufferings. She then had recourse, as was her custom, to the patronage of the most Blessed Virgin, and calling D. Scolastica, she asked her to place a pious image upon her eyes. And the fact was, that

at the very touch every vestige of the obstinate
humour immediately disappeared.

Finally she cherished an especial affection for
the patriarch St. Joseph, the chaste Spouse of
Mary, for her Angel Guardian, St. Ignatius of
Lyola, St. Francis Xavier, and the holy Virgins SS. Ursula, Gertrude and Teresa of Jesus.
Above all she was extremely devout to St.
Catharine of Sienna, whom she purposed speci-
ally to imitate, as St. Rose of Lima, her model,
had done, and she knew her whole life so well
by heart that she could point out and relate the
smallest incident mentioned in it. An attentive
reading of the lives of her patron Saints, in
order to imitate them, was one of her most
pleasing and ordinary occupations. True it is,
that when in the course of her reading she
chanced to come across extraordinary and supernatural graces, and especially when she read
of visions and revelations she passed them by,
saying, that such things were not for her, who
ought to walk in an humble and lowly path, and
attend only to the acquisition of solid virtue.
And this much will suffice to prove what we
asserted at the heading of this chapter.

CHAPTER XIII.

THE ZEAL OF THE BLESSED MARY ANN FOR THE
SALVATION OF SOULS.   HER STRATAGEMS TO
BRING BACK TO A BETTER LIFE THOSE WHO HAD
GONE ASTRAY.   REMARKABLE CONVERSION OF A
NOBLE INDIAN LADY.   HER CHARITY TO RELIEVE
THE TEMPORAL WANTS OF HER NEIGHBOUR CON-
FIRMED BY ALMIGHTY GOD WITH MIRACLES.

A LIFE wholly devoted to recollection, to
prayer, to the interiour culture of the soul, such
as we have hitherto described in that of the
Blessed Mary Ann of Jesus, may seem that it
might not, or would not have leisure or time,
and perhaps not even the inclination to labour
for the good of others. But as true charity
towards God is never separated from a sincere
love towards our neighbour, so it is peculiar to
those who are truly pious, as was the case with
Mary Ann, to make use of every exertion and
means to procure advantage to others, according to their state and condition in life. She
was not content with the prayers and penances
which she offered up every day to God for the
conversion of infidels, heretics and sinners of

18

every description, but she actively interested
herself in it to gain these objects.

And commencing with the household, she first
of all took charge of the servants, teaching them
the mysteries of faith, and diligently instructing
them in every thing which regarded the obliga-
tions and duties of a Christian life.   After this,
by her winning manners, she induced both masters and servants to frequent the holy Sacraments of confession and communion every Sunday and solemn festival of the year; a thing
very rare in those days, and therefore doubly
difficult for her to bring about.   The day before
she herself informed them that the day following would be the day for communion; and the
better to prepare the more ignorant of the
family, she would assemble them all together,
and make them fervourous exhortations, exercising them in lively acts of faith, hope and
charity.   When she chanced to discover any
grievous fault committed by any one of the
house, after weeping over it before God and
severely punishing it in herself, she undertook
to repair it, correcting the guilty one with such
love, and at the same time so effectually, that
she drew from them sentiments of compunction
and resolutions of amendment.   It may be seen

from a single fact, which I shall here relate,
how much she strove to bring back to the path
of duty the souls of her domestics.

Mary Ann had taken into her service a poor
young girl, more for the sake of preserving her
from the many dangers to which she was exposed
than that she had any need of her; and she endeavoured to improve her heart and instil into
it lively sentiments of piety. But the girl, although she had continually before her eyes
bright examples of virtue, instigated by the
devil and her passions, suffered herself to be
drawn away from her good resolutions and fell
into a serious fault; and at the same time conceived such an aversion, and as it were hatred,
for her mistress that, unable to endure the idea
of appearing before her again, thought about
abandoning her and of flying away secretly.
Wherefore, one night, after getting every thing
ready for her intended flight, she was already
on her way in the dark towards the staircase,
when whom should she meet but Mary Ann,
who had come out of her apartment contrary to
her usual custom, and who requested her to get
her a light and come along with her. The girl
obeyed, and artfully dissembling her artifice,
followed her mistress, who, when she was come

into her room, made her sit down by her side,
and in the kindest manner asked her why she
was so interiourly disturbed, and whither she
thought about going at that late hour? It
would seem but natural, that seeing the guilty
intention which was concealed in her mind, and
which was known to none but God, discovered,
it would have been sufficient to have brought
her back to her right senses: but the fact was,
that becoming worse at such a manifestation of
the divine mercy, she obstinately denied every
thing, and merely said that she was unable to
continue longer in her service. Then Mary Ann
spoke in plainer terms, telling her that she
should reflect well on the step she was about to
take, and not suffer herself to be blinded by
passion: that she should beware of that which
is the consequence of sin, viz anxiety of mind,
remorse of conscience, enmity with God, eternal
sufferings; that she had always loved her as her
daughter, and that she did not deserve, after all
the marks of love she had shown her, to be so
vilely abandoned by her. She then embraced
her with many expressions of affection, and
said, "Ah, why will you then abandon me?
Why will you forsake me?" The girl was
moved at such manifestation of affection, but

not changed in mind; and that very same night,
doing violence to herself, she left the house and
miserably abandoned herself to a licentious and
dissolute life. It was well for her that her kind
mistress never ceased to offer up her prayers
and penances to Almighty God, till at last she
obtained her sincere conversion, as she herself
afterwards deposed to the glory, as well as in
gratitude for the charity, of Mary Ann.

The efficacy of the prayers and words of the
servant of God was so well known throughout
the city, that to overcome the obstinacy of the
most hardened sinners they recurred to her as
to their last resort. A young man who had led
a very bad and scandalous life, fell grievously
sick, lost the use of his senses, and was dying
in the public hospital, without being able to
make his confession. Mary Ann was informed
of the dangerous state of his soul; and she after
a short prayer obtained for him the recovery of
his senses, to enable him to receive the last
Sacraments, which he did with sentiments of
true compunction, and then departed this life.
An Indian woman also, by name of Giovanna di
Sanguera, a Moor by birth and a slave by condition, found in Mary Ann a remedy and an
escape from a wretched life and a worse death,

18*

which her barbarous husband wished to inflict
on her. He ran about like a madman in search
of his wife to kill her, and having understood
that she was hearing mass in the church of the
Jesuits, he went thither immediately, carrying
a dagger in his hand. His wife no sooner perceived him coming in, than reasonably fearing
for her life, she ran to place herself near the
servant of God, imploring her assistance and
mercy. Mary Ann immediately rose to her
feet, and advancing towards the savage wretch,
said to him in a gentle tone, "Calm yourself, O
son. What are you thinking to do with that
dagger? Do you not see the horrible crime
which you are about to perpetrate?" And she
went on blending so much sweetness and charity
with her words, at one time reprehending for
his sacriligious attempt, then persuading him to
enter into himself, that she succeeded in calm-
ing his fury, and causing him to become as meek
as a lamb. After this she comforted the still
trembling woman, and told her to lay aside all
fear and return home, because from thenceforward she would never have the least occasion
of complaint against her husband, as in fact it
turned out.

More remarkable still was the change effected

in D. Maria Duchizela, who, after leading a
loose and unconstrained life, became very modest
and religious. She was an Indian by birth, but
of the most noble blood, being a descendant of
the royal family of the Incas, who once governed
the country round Quito. She was very punc-
tilious in point of honour, and being proud of
her beauty and the abundance of her earthly
goods, she exhibited more pomp and show than
if she were really a queen. Being come to Quito
for the purpose of settling some disputes in the
tribunal of the Royal Audience, she chanced,
upon a certain festival to hear mass in the
chapel of our Lady of the Angels, which was
opposite, as we said, the house of Mary Ann.
The exteriour of the young lady was one of
pride, her dress was of the most costly material,
her head and neck were adorned with flowers,
gold and pearls, and the very air was impreg-
nated around her with perfumes and sweet
odours. She seemed to have come thither for
the purpose of attracting attention, and not for
paying her adoration to her God. By good luck
Mary Ann was passing by the chapel, on her
way to the church of the Jesuits, and hearing
the sound of the little bell, at the time of the
elevation, immediately stopped and knelt down

near D. Maria, whom she had never known or
seen before, and continued praying till the end
of mass. And when this was over she turned
to the young lady, and in the sweetest manner
asked her name and whence she came. The
other with equal affability told her that her
name was Maria, that she came from Parequis,
her native place, whither she would return in
the course of fifteen days. Then Mary Ann
seizing the good opportunity replied, that "she
congratulated her upon the beautiful name that
had fallen to her lot; that she should consequently strive to nourish a special devotion to
the Queen of Angels, endeavouring to imitate
her virtues. Above all, she should beware of
wasting and throwing away such endowments
of beauty and mind with which she had been
enriched, but should rather consecrate them to
God, studying to please him alone and not the
world, which is a traitor and abandons us in our
greatest need. As to your returning to your
country after fifteen days," she added with a
smile, "perhaps, Signora, it may not be so: the
most Blessed Virgin will inform you." Having
said this, she courteously saluted her and took
her leave. The affability and modesty of the
servant of God so gained upon the heart of D.

Maria, that she was hardly gone before she
asked those near her who that person was; and
having been informed that she was Mary Ann
of Jesus, a most innocent and holy virgin, of
whom she had heard so many things by report,
she burnt with a desire of seeing her again, and
of becoming better acquainted with her; and
immediately went in pursuit of her to the church
of the Jesuits, and placing herself at her side,
whispered to her " to be pleased to recommend
her to God." Mary Ann replied that " she had
already done so, and would do so again: in the
meantime," she added, " let your ladyship open
your ears to the interiour voice by which Almighty God calls you to his service." This was
the second and last time she spoke to her, for
the servant of God shortly after fell sick and
died: but her words remained so deeply engraven upon the heart of the lady, that, as she
herself afterwards confessed, they were the
cause of her renouncing every vanity of the
world, and of giving herself entirely to God.
Nor was the sacrifice small which it cost her to
carry out her good resolution; for from a state
of opulence she was reduced to almost absolute
beggary, and had to break off, at the same time,
so many dangerous friendships contracted, live

far away from her native land, abandon her
relatives, and renounce all the advantages and
conveniences of life. She generously trampled
under foot every worldly consideration; despised
the honours and vanities of the world, overcome
all opposition, and triumphed over her very
nature, for from being of a very haughty and
choleric disposition, which would sometimes
cause her to faint and lose the use of her senses
through excess of anger, she became in this
regard, by the continual practice of mortification, as one that was insensible and dead. She
never returned to her country, as it had been
foretold her; but following the counsel given
her by Mary Ann of Jesus, to place herself
under the direction of the Fathers of the Society
of Jesus, towards whom she at first felt. without
knowing why, a natural aversion, she continued
in Quito to her death, and led a truly exemplary
and holy life. Not content with that, in order
to repair the scandals which she had given, she
took upon herself the care of collecting poor,
orphan and destitute girls, whose virtue was
endangered, and having given an asylum to
forty of them in her own house, she maintained
them all on the alms she begged from the pious,
on the profit which she drew from the labour

of her own hands, and carefully instructed them
in Christian piety and good morals. Finally,
in the many and frequent misfortunes of poverty,
sickness and persecutions which she encountered, she found no better aid than by recurring
to the intercession of Mary Ann, then happy in
heaven, and receiving from her comfort and
succour even with evident and stupendous miracles, which would require too much of our time
to relate here in detail.

For the sake of brevity I pass over other facts
in proof of the zeal which our Saint had for
the salvation of souls; and I come now to say
something of her compassion for the corporal
necessities of her neighbours. From the time
she was a little child, as was said before, there
was nothing that pleased her more than to distribute with her own hand alms to the poor,
who came every day to the door of the house.
And her parents, who were inclined to assist the
poor, delighted to observe in their daughter the
same desire, furnished her every day with an
abundance of bread to distribute amongst the
poor. And she did it with such a grace and interiour joy of soul, that afterwards, when she
came to live in the house of her sister, she not
only did not leave off this charitable occupation,

but added to it. For besides teaching the first
rudiments of the Christian doctrine to all those
miserable beings, who assembled every day to
receive alms from her, she took the most filthy
and ragged of them aside, and with her own
hands fixed their dress, cleaned and combed
them. It was certainly a moving spectacle, and
many came to witness it, to behold a young lady,
belonging to one of the first families, well edu-
cated and refined, whose very nature abhorred
every species of uncleanness, exercising herself
with so much love, as if she were a maid-servant,
in those vile and low offices, besides being
loathsome, and generously overcoming every
natural repugnance.

From the time she consecrated herself to God
by vows, and became voluntarily poor for the
love · of God, she could never dispose of any
thing as her own: but as charity is wonderfully
industrious, it taught her the way of strictly
observing her vow of poverty, and at the same
time of showing herself liberal and generous to
the poor. She asked and obtained permission
of her relatives to bestow every day that portion of food which would have fallen to her
share, and which she never eat. Besides this,
all the profit which she gained from the labour

of her hands, she distributed, with the consent
of her confessor, among the poor, and especially
to the bashful, or to families that were once in
easy circumstances but then reduced. In like
manner she maintained for several years some
destitute widows, several little girls who were
in danger, and a good priest who had lost the
use of reason in consequence of the poison
given him to drink by the infidels, among whom
he had laboured, and who had been brought
back to Quito and was living in extreme want.
Wherefore the needy of every description con-
fidently applied to Mary Ann as to their mother;
and in order not to disturb her during the day
from her usual exercises of devotion, they were
accustomed, from the public street, to throw a
pebble at the shutter of a window, which overlooked a less frequented alley, and which she
always purposely kept closed. This was sufficient to make her cast down immediately to the
poor whatever might happen to come to her hand.

It happened not unfrequently that God concurred to stamp the charity of his servant with
manifest prodigies, a few of which I shall here
set down. It would frequently occur, that after
having distributed to the poor all that had been
assigned by the family for them, either new

comers would arrive, or on account of the very
great number, not a few would remain, who had
been unable to obtain any thing. Mary Ann
was sensibly afflicted; and her compassionate
heart not suffering her to send any one away
empty-handed, full of confidence she was seen
to re-enter her apartment, and after a short time
come forth again with a basket full of the whitest bread in her hand. The domestics frequently
witnessed this and agreed together to watch
attentively and see who brought her the bread.
But all their diligence was to no purpose: and
they were obliged to conclude that God miraculously furnished it.

Whenever they made bread at home, our
Saint hastened to give her labour, wishing with
her own hands to knead a certain quantity,
which she afterwards distributed to a poor
family, consisting of three marriageable daughters, in whom she took much interest, on account
of the danger in which they were of going
astray, from the extreme poverty to which they
were reduced. She never ceased from her la-
borious task, notwithstanding the opposition of
the domestics, who considered such a drudgery
unbefitting her. After having, together with
them, kneaded the dough, she took from the

mass a small quantity, which, as the witnesses affirmed, scarcely weighed about two ounces; and she worked it so that she formed of it a loaf more perfect and whiter than the rest, and when it was baked it weighed at least thirty ounces. At first those of the house were filled with wonder, but afterwards seeing the same thing occurring every time, they spoke of it as a continued and ordinary prodigy, and therefore it no longer excited any surprise in them.

The following fact is also confirmed in the juridical depositions. Her brother-in-law, as well as her sister, had many times given to Mary Ann full power to take from the dispensary and granary whatever she wanted for the relief of the poor: and the servant of God, availing herself of this pious liberality of her relatives, frequently took from the one and the other place abundant alms. After some time their curiosity was excited to see how much she took, but in spite of all their scrutiny they could never perceive that a single particle of any thing was missed. At which D. Cosimo mildly expostulated with her, as if she doubted the sincerity by which he and his wife gave her full liberty to use their property as she chose for the benefit of the poor. Mary Ann replied to

him in a very bland and gay manner, and told
him to "give himself no uneasiness on this account, for she and her poor were well satisfied
with their charity; that in the meantime he
should return thanks to Almighty God, if in
recompense of their charity they missed nothing." This much she said, and then was silent.
This was enough to show that God by a miracle
replaced that quantity, which his servant had
taken, as necessity required, and distributed to
the needy.

CHAPTER XIV.

SUPERNATURAL GIFTS IMPARTED TO THE BLESSED
MARY ANN BY ALMIGHTY GOD. SHE SEES HIDDEN
AND DISTANT THINGS, AND PREDICTS THE FUTURE.
SHE MIRACULOUSLY HEALS MANY PERSONS OF
MORTAL DISTEMPERS AND RECALLS A DEAD
WOMAN TO LIFE.

THESE were not the only acts of Mary Ann
which surpassed the bounds of nature, and by
which it pleased Almighty God to illustrate her
name and honour her merits and sanctity. Although she continually asked of him the grace
of never being privileged or distinguished with

extraordinary gifts and favours of this kind; nevertheless Almighty God, as a reward for such humility, and for the glory of his sacred name, frequently wished to exalt her in the eyes of men; and besides these instances which we have already mentioned, the following may serve as a confirmation.

Our Saint had hardly passed to a better life than D. Giovanna, her niece, immediately recollected every thing that had been told her, when Mary Ann, by order of her confessor, had unfolded to her the inmost secrets of her soul. Among the other things, one was that Jesus Christ frequently allowed himself to be seen by her in the consecrated host, under the appearance of a lovely Infant, filling her with unspeakable joy; and that sometimes she tasted the ineffable delights of paradise, when she received holy communion, it seeming to her that she sensibly received the holy Infant within her heart.

Besides this, she had the gift of seeing hidden and distant things, as if they were under her eyes and present, as also of pronouncing with uncertainty on the future events. Many facts of this kind are related in the process of beatification, some few of which it will be sufficient for me to select as specimens of the rest; and I

shall have more regard for variety than any
particular arrangement of facts. She wrote a
letter to Father Antonio Monosalvas, who was
at the time in Riobamba, a city about thirty
leagues distant from Quito, and in it she said to
him: "That knowing for certain that he was
shortly to come to Quito, she took the liberty
of sending him a small quantity of biscuits to
serve for his journey." There was then no reason, nor any order why the Father should depart thence; but a few days afterwards a very
serious accident occurred, on account of which
the city council deliberated about sending a wise
and prudent person to Quito to transact their
business, and by common consent the choice fell
upon Father Monosalvas, who had scarcely
reached the capital before he went to see Mary
Ann, and wished to know from her how she obtained the information of his unexpected desti-
nation. She told him frankly as to her confessor: "My Divine Spouse knows every thing,
and he also knew of your coming here. From
him I had the information, and therefore I sent
to your Reverence that small quantity of biscuit." Thus she spoke, and she added: "that
when he would have returned to Riobamba he
would have to undergo a very severe tribula-

tion, but that he should not be afraid, for God would soon console him, as in fact it happened, and as he himself testified in the juridical process.

Antonio de Paz being mortally wounded, Catharine his mother ran immediately to the servant of God, both to inform her of the sad accident as well as to receive from her some consolation and comfort. But scarcely had Mary Ann seen her than suddenly with great commiseration. " I know already," said she, "why you come: but there is no time to be lost: make him go to confession immediately and receive the last Sacraments, as he will soon die; and let this misfortune be to you an exercise of much patience, and an entire resignation to the will of God." After hearing this the disconsolate mother quickly returned home and frankly told the reply of Mary Ann to the sick man: and he, without more ado, prepared himself for death with true sentiments of Christian piety. As soon as he was dead Catharine went again to the servant of God, but the hour being late, and finding the doors of the house already closed, she threw a pebble at the window, at which Mary Ann immediately made her appearance, and before the other could speak—"I know already, Catharine," said she, "that you come pierced with grief for the death of Antonio your son. But don't afflict yourself, rather give many thanks to the Lord, because he is in a place of safety."

Still more wonderful, on account of the circumstances connected with it, was the prediction which she made of his approaching death, to a man in the bloom of health and of a perfectly sound constitution. This man having for several years led a dissolute life, at last being ashamed of himself, desired to rise from the state of sin, but from the habit which he had contracted did not know how to come to the resolution of breaking off at once the occasion of it. By good luck God put it into his heart to have recourse to Mary Ann; and having waited for her one morning when she was going to the church, with all humility and candour he explained to her his need, and prayed her to be pleased to recommend him to God. She replied that she would do so willingly, and promised to offer up her holy communion for him that very mo ning. When on her return home, a little before noon, she chanced to meet that poor miserable man in the street again, who asked her, if she had obtained the grace for him which he desired?

She then raised her eyes to heaven, and standing for some time recollected, told him these precise words: "Sir, although I feel a delicacy in speaking, nevertheless, as it too nearly concerns your eternal salvation, I will speak with all sincerity. Prepare yourself without delay to die, for within eight days you shall have rendered an account of your life to Jesus Christ." The man was thunder struck to hear such an unexpected intimation; afterwards taking courage, he returned to his own home, where, being suddenly seized with a mortal distemper, he survived precisely eight days, which he spent in continual tears and acts of sincere repentance, when, having received the last Sacraments, he died with great signs of predestination.

In the same manner she predicted to Catharine Peralto, a little girl of six years of age, and daughter of D. Giovanna her niece, that she would never marry, because God wished her for himself, and destined her for a life of no ordinary sanctity: as it afterwards turned out, in spite of the opposition of her father, who persisted in his resolution to give her a husband, and had already made all the necessary preparations. She took the religious habit among the bare-footed Carmelites, where she lived and died in the odour of sanctity. D. Giovanna had another son by name of Cosimo; the very one who, as we said before, saw Mary Ann with the Infant Jesus in her arms. Being of an extremely lively and restless disposition, and fearing one day for some childish fault he had committed, of being chastised by his father, he fled for protection into Mary Ann's apartment which by chance he found open. The father overtook him there, and would have punished him on the spot, had not the servant of God interposed by telling him that Cosimo would one day become quite a different person, and she went security for him. And the fact was, that the youth, as if he had changed his nature, became very grave and sedate, and a few years afterwards, bidding adieu to the world, he entered and lived a Religious in the Society of Jesus.

It would take too long were I to relate, one by one, the predictions made by the Blessed Mary Ann, which are deposed at length in the process of beatification. I cannot be silent here of one which was celebrated all over the city of Quito, and which was moreover accompanied with so many and such prodigious circumstances, that on this account also it is worthy to be known. One day Mary Ann was returning from

the church in company with her nieces, and they
had gone but a few steps when the rain began
to fall in torrents. Her companions, in order to
protect themselves the best way they could, got
close to the wall, under the eves of the houses,
and hastened their steps to procure shelter. But
the servant of God, who was engrossed all the
while in heavenly things, as if she were perfectly unconscious of what was passing around
her, proceeded slowly along in the middle of the
street, where there was a complete deluge which
poured down in torrents from the roofs of the
houses. When she entered the hall of the house,
where her nieces, all wet and disordered, awaited
her, her clothes as well as her feet appeared to
be perfectly dry, although she had to walk in
the midst of the torrent, which rushed down the
declivity of the street. At the sight of her they
looked at each other in amazement; and at the
same time Mary Ann, becoming aware of their
surprise, and still more of the prodigy which she
could not conceal, anticipated them, saying with
a sweet smile: "'Tis well; you are wet because
you did not know how to walk. How is it? I
have not had a single drop of water upon me,
and you are so wet?" "But we had not," replied one of them, "as you, an angel who de-

fended us from the rain." Mary Ann blushed
and quickly changed the conversation: but without being conscious of it, from one prodigy she
passed to another, which was probably greater:
for leaning against a little pillar, as if in the act
of resting herself, "this house," said she, "will
one day be the dwelling and monastery of bare-
footed Carmelites, nuns:" then going up stairs
she invited her companions to accompany her
through the house, and like one entranced,
pointing now to one place, now to another,
"here," she added, "will be the gate of the
monastery, there the refectory and the kitchen;
the church will be built on this side which faces
the street; and the rooms which I occupy will
be the choir. Oh, with what pleasure will the
Carmelite nuns dwell in this place!" When she
had said this she took her leave and shut herself up in her apartment. It would take too
long to recount how, notwithstanding all the
difficulties which were met with, a few years
after her death, the words of Mary Ann were
verified to the very letter. Suffice it to say,
that some of her nieces were eye-witnesses of
the fact, having become nuns in the very same
monastery.

Many wonderful things are likewise related

in the juridical processes, which Almighty God
operated by the prayers and the touch of Mary
Ann, whilst she was still alive. She cured, in
an instant, two of her nieces who were mortally
sick, by only giving them to drink a sip of pure
water. Another lady was suffering severely
from a sore in her foot, which was beginning to
mortify. She had herself brought from her
country-seat where she dwelt, into the city and
implored the assistance of Mary Ann. She only
wet the sore with her saliva, and it was all that
was required, for in a short time it was perfectly healed. She twice delivered her sister,
D. Girolama, from imminent danger of death in
two difficult cases of child-birth. D. Giovanna,
niece of the servant of God, being obliged to
leave the city for a short time, left in her charge
a little daughter of three years of age, who,
whilst playing in the court-yard, received such
a terrible kick in the face from a mule that
bruised and wounded, it fell to the ground without giving any signs of life. Mary Ann being
informed of it immediately raised her eyes to
heaven and said: "Oh, what account shall I
give of this child to its parents?" She ordered
her Indian servant to bring the child into her
room, and shutting herself up, she remained in

prayer for about an hour; after that she came
forth carrying the child in her arms perfectly
sound, with only a very small scar remaining
on the forehead where it had been struck.

Maria de Paredes deposed in the process the
instantaneous cure of one of her daughters, in
the following terms:—"Eleonora, daughter of
the deponent, having fallen sick, and her life
being entirely despaired of by the physicians,
the deponent went with tears in her eyes to
Mary Ann, to beg her to recommend her little
daughter to God: and she consoled her with
telling her not to be afflicted, for it would be
nothing, and that she should give her a beverage
composed of the dried leaves of roses, which
had been upon the body of St. Rose of Lima:
and having sent it, she gave it to the invalid to
drink, who immediately recovered, and was so
thoroughly cured, that from that time she never
felt any symptom of her former disease."

Maria Rodriguez likewise attested under oath,
" that an Indian woman, by the name of Beatrix,
a slave of Giovanni Salazar, being in great danger from the labours of child-birth, in the house
of the servant of God, Mary Ann of Jesus, the
same Mary Ann came down to pay her a visit,
and putting her hand on the head of the sufferer.

said :—' May it please the Lord to rescue you
from this danger.' And hardly had she pronounced the words before the Indian was happily
delivered. The child was immediately baptised,
and afterwards died the same day. D. Giovanna
di Casso, her niece, wished to inform the servant
of God of it, and said to her, that the little
negro was dead, for which she had stood sponsor:
to whom Mary Ann replied, ' that it was born
for heaven, and therefore God had taken it to
himself.' "

Giovanna Peralta fell sick of a malignant
fever; and after being reduced to the last extremity was visited by the Blessed Mary Ann,
her relative, who, after consoling her with pious
discourse, when on the point of leaving, " Courage," said she, " be of good heart, as you will
not only not die of this sickness, but survive me
a good while." The disease, however, instead
of diminishing, became so alarming that Catharine, in order not to be present at the death of
her sister, left the house and went to the church
of the Jesuits, where she found the servant of
God, who again confirmed what she had already
said in regard to the cure of the sick person.
But Catharine giving little credit to it, asked
her boldly how she could make her that promise

with so much assurance? And she replied, "I can, on the premise the most Holy Virgin has made me." Catharine, hearing this reply, returned immediately home, and, to her great surprise, found her sister not only free from the fever but perfectly cured.

I shall close this chapter with the relation of a still more wonderful fact, which is to be found in the process. Two Indians, a man and his wife, lived in the house of Mary Ann; and for some time they lived happily and amicably together. After some years the husband having conceived an unjust and false suspicion of his wife, like a brute as he really was, determined without more ado to kill her. Wherefore, under pretence of being obliged to cut wood, he took her with him to a mountain near Quito, and there, in the heart of the forest, bound her tightly to a tree, and having beaten her unmercifully with a knotted club, he put a halter round her neck, strangled her, and threw the corpse down a precipice from a high rock, in order to conceal for ever all traces of his crime. Mary Ann, wrapt in spirit, saw from her room all that had taken place in the distant woods. Calling to her a good tradesman, who kept his shop under her window, she begged him to go immediately to the mountain, where, concealed by a certain cliff, which she pointed out, he would find a dead woman; and to take her up and convey her with all possible secrecy there to her room. The man obeyed; and as soon as Mary Ann had possession of the lacerated and bloody corpse, she raised her eyes to heaven, and applied to the throat, and the other affected parts, some rose leaves; and the Indian instantly began to breathe, and shortly after got up perfectly cured, with no other mark remaining except a very slight impression of the halter with which she had been strangled. The fact was soon spread abroad: and the nieces of the Saint interrogated the Indian to discover the truth. But she was unable to say more than that finding herself in the agonies of death, she seemed to see, as in a dream, Mary Ann of Jesus making towards her and promising assistance and succour.

CHAPTER XV.

THE INVINCIBLE PATIENCE AND PERFECT RESIGNA·
TION OF THE BLESSED MARY ANN IN HER LONG
AND PAINFUL INFIRMITIES.   HER HEROIC FORTI·
TUDE IN MORTIFYING HER THIRST REWARDED BY
ALMIGHTY GOD WITH MIRACLES.

It will not be disagreeable to the reader, if
before I proceed to give an account of the
Blessed Mary Ann's precious death, I should
set forth in this chapter and place before his
eyes the wonderful examples, which she has left
us, of perfect resignation and heroic patience in
the course of her long and painful infirmities.
She had to suffer much, especially during the
last seven years of her life, from prostration of
strength, fainting fits, swoons, burning fevers,
and in the end from dropsy accompanied with
dangerous symptoms.   The pains alone of her
stomach, which not unfrequently assailed her,
were so acute and excessive that she herself did
rot hesitate to affirm in confidence to Father
Fra. Girolama, her brother, and to Father Camaccio her confessor, that they would without
doubt have deprived her of life, had they lasted

out for one full quarter of an hour. Notwithstanding all this, whether sick or well, she always maintained the same joyful and serene
countenance, always the same sweetness and
affability of manners. She continued as before
to practice her ordinary penances, and to follow
in every thing the distribution of time prescribed for her daily exercises. She could never
be induced to take to her bed and put herself
under the care of physicians, except when there
was danger of death, or when she could no
longer stand upon her feet. And on these occasions no one ever heard a single word of complaint, or a sigh indicative of the great sufferings which she endured—nay, the more her
pains increased, the greater was her joy and
exultation. She said that these were all so
many caresses and delights sent her by her heavenly Spouse, and consequently that she was
really blessed, because without any merit of her
own she was made worthy of the divine compla-
cency.

As sufferings and infirmities were esteemed
by her as extraordinary graces and favours, we
need not wonder if she changed them i.   nd
made them sources of enjoyment, in s   h   as
to desire always to suffer more and m   e f   the

love of her God. Being one day very much
tormented with her pains, she threw herself into
the arms of Maria Arias, her particular friend,
and as if seeking for some relief, begged her to
strike her with her hand between the shoulders,
pretending that she felt some numbness there.
The other obliged, firmly believing that she was
alleviating her pains by so doing; but the truth
was that she increased them beyond measure, as
the servant of God had desired; for precisely in
that part she had a frightful iron chain, the
points of which were so embeded by the blows
in her flesh that the physicians afterwards could
with difficulty draw them out without tearing
the flesh.

But where her heroic patience and mortification shine most conspicuous was in her last sickness, which was dropsy, and which afflicted her
for many years. One of the ordinary effects of
this disease is wont to be, as every body knows,
an excessive and morbid thirst, which can never
be allayed. Now Mary Ann, who never in the
whole course of her life used any other beverage
except pure water, and that also sparingly, when
she was attacked by this new disease, and therefore stood in greater need than ever of quenching her thirst oftener, abstained on the contrary

more than ever from drink, in order to mortify
the burning thirst with which she was consumed.
It would seem perfectly incredible, but it is a
fact which rests on the testimony of many witnesses, that she passed entire weeks. and once
went as far as three months without tasting a
drop of water. And if she did not die, as was
but natural, of pure thirst, it was the grace and
power of God which supported her life.

Great, therefore, was the torment which she
endured; but the more acute and distressing it
was, the dearer it was always to her. The very
sight of water excited in her parched and burning body the most violent contortions, caused
by the great desire which afflicted humanity felt
to seek some refreshment. Notwithstanding all
this, Mary Ann not only with heroic fortitude
repressed every propensity and craving of nature, but to render her martyrdom more excruciating and her mortification more excessive, she
would go to the bucket of water which she
always kept in her rooms for this purpose, and
filling a small vase she held it up before her
eyes, and then slowly and little by little poured
it back into the bucket. She was observed to
do the same thing at a fountain, taking up the
limped water, and then turn round and throw

it back into the basin. At the noise which the rain made in falling, the parched child would extend her body out of the window, and with her eyes and face turned towards heaven would give a thousand praises and thanks to God, for giving her that fine opportunity of mortifying her thirst. At other times making a cup of the hollow of her hands, she collected the rain which fell from the eaves of the roof; after that, opening them on a sudden, she let the water fall to the ground, as if offering it in sacrifice to God, in imitation of the holy prophet David. She was once surprised in this act by a lady who lived opposite to her dwelling, and who could not refrain from asking her for what purpose she stood admiring and collecting the water, if afterwards she made no use of it to quench her thirst? And the servant of God, blushing for shame, quietly replied that she did so to mortify herself a little, and then suddenly withdrew to her room. Another time being parched with thirst, and hearing the gurgling sound of a freshet, which ran in torrents through the streets from the late rains, with a sudden motion she exclaimed with a sigh—"Oh, that one could plunge herself into that water to allay a little her burning thirst!" A lady hearing this who was present offered her immediately a glass of fresh water; but Mary Ann humbly thanking her for her charity refused the offering, and added: "because that exclamation escaped me, you must not imagine, madam, that I would drink this water. Think rather that I feel a real pleasure in associating in his last moments with my languishing Spouse, who, tormented also with thirst, died for me upon the cross." And if she was sometimes compelled by obedience or by extreme necessity to take a few sips of water, or to keep it a little while in her mouth to moisten her throat, she mixed so much gall and bitter substances with it that she rendered the taste of it intolerable. During the last day of her life, when she was very ill, she manifested her desire for a few fresh grapes. After much search a small bunch was found and brought to her; but she to irritate rather than for the sake of quenching her thirst, took but three single grapes, and then absolutely refused the remainder.

It happened sometimes that her dry and parched throat would become contracted and tightly closed for the want of necessary moisture: and then the only remedy she adopted, was to put little pieces of apple in her mouth and ex-

tract the juice. She did not very often use this
mode of relief, on the contrary she very often
refused it, or turned it to her greater mortification. She would take in her hand the finest
looking and the best flavoured of the apples
which were given her, look at them wistfully,
and then hand them to her nieces, praying them
to eat them in her presence, and thus cruelly torment her burning thirst with the sight of them
eating. So great virtue merited to be rewarded
by Almighty God with stupendous prodigies, one
of which only I will here relate, as I find it deposed in the process. One day her confessor
ordered Mary Ann that she should not taste a
sip of drink of any kind for fifteen consecutive
days. His intention was to see what impression
a command so strange and contrary to all rules
of prudence would make upon her, and what
emotions and thoughts it would excite in her
mind and heart; and then an hour after, when
she would return to make her confession, he in-
timated to revoke the order, nay, to oblige her
to take more frequent nourishment. But God,
who wished to give us another example of her
heroic obedience and perfect resignation, arranged it so that he forgot every thing about it.
The obedient Mary Ann, without stopping to

reflect on the command she received, joyfully
prepared herself to execute it to the very letter;
and as for some days previous she had taken no
refreshment, she began soon to feel all the
dreadful effects and torments of a burning thirst.
She could have easily rid herself of this suffering
by merely stating her case to her confessor; but
fearing to lose by so doing the merit of obedience, she was silent, and although every morning and frequently during the day she returned
to see him, she never said a word to him about
it.   And she was on the very point of failing
and of being reduced to the last extremity, when
God, satisfied with the display of so much virtue, miraculously comforted and sustained her.
A very heavy rain was falling; and Mary Ann,
who felt an interiour anguish, went to the window and held out both hands joined together to
catch the rain which fell, and afterwards to
make of it, as was her custom, a pleasing holocaust, by throwing it on the ground without
tasting a drop of it   No sooner however were
the palms of both hands filled, than as if they
had been a sponge, they miraculously imbibed
and absorbed all the water she had collected.
This happened to her great surprise, not once,
but as long as she kept her hands extended, and

she felt her whole interiour cooled and her
burning cease.

———•←———

CHAPTER XVI.

THE GREAT DESIRE WHICH THE BLESSED MARY ANN
HAD OF DEATH. SHE OFFERS HERSELF TO GOD
AS A VICTIM FOR THE PRESERVATION OF HER
FELLOW-CITIZENS AND FALLS GRIEVOUSLY SICK.
RECEIVES WITH THE MOST TENDER AFFECTION
THE LAST SACRAMENTS, AND EXPIRES IN THE
ARMS OF JESUS AND MARY, WHO DESCENDED
FROM HEAVEN TO RECEIVE HER SOUL, WHOSE
GLORY IS REVEALED TO BROTHER FERDINANDO
DELLA CROCE.

A SOUL so disengaged from the things here
below could not but pant with an ardent desire
of flying quickly to the bosom of its God. Every
time the conversation turned on death, the
Blessed Mary Ann was observed to manifest
the greatest joy, and her whole countenance to
brighten with extraordinary consolation. The
very sickness, the pains and the spasms of her
body were also on this account unspeakably dear
to her: for she hoped that at last they would so
diminish her strength as to render her recovery

hopeless. Hence the many sighs and tears she shed, as if she had no greater pain than that of living, nor expected a greater grace than that of dying.

Thus she went on animating her hopes till the beginning of the year 1645, when it seemed she had by a supernatural light some certainty of her approaching dissolution. She began from that time to speak of it, at first obscurely, and afterwards in terms sufficiently clear to several of her more confidential friends. Moreover, the wonderful death which we have related in another place of D. Sebastiana her niece, which happened about this time, revived the desire of following her, and of speedily uniting herself to her in heaven. Likewise not a few, on the testimony of her confessors, deposed in the juridical process that in that secret colloquy which she had with her dying niece, she not only revealed to her the glory prepared for her in heaven, but added, that she should prepare the place for her, as she would follow her in a short time. The truth is, that but a few months intervened between the death of Sebastiana and that of Mary Ann. As therefore the twenty-six years, which Mary Ann spent upon this earth, were but a life of a continued sacrifice, so the

Lord was pleased that the last act of it should
be in reality a holocaust, in virtue of which she
offered herself up as a victim of charity for the
relief and preservation of her fellow-citizens.
The thing happened in this manner:—

In the year 1645 America was visited by a
contagious disease, which laid waste many of
the southern provinces. It made its appearance
also in the city of Quito, and in a short time it
spread itself, committing the most terrible
havoc among every class of citizens, who daily
fell victims to its fury. The churches and ceme-
teries were insufficient to contain the great number of the dead, and heaps of abandoned and
unburied corpses were seen in the streets and in
the environs of the city. To increase the universal dread frequent earthquakes were felt,
which shook and overturned many villages and
populous cities. Every body was in tears, in
mourning and in confusion. It happened that
on the 25th of March Father Alfonso Roxas,
Mary Ann's confessor, was explaining the sacred
scripture in the church of the Society, and at
the end of his discourse, after describing, with
much eloquence, the ruins of the city of Riobamba, that had just been destroyed by an
earthquake he exhorted the people in strong

language to implore mercy and pardon of Almighty God, and to do penance, in order to avert those tremendous chastisements of the divine justice: after this, inflamed with an ardent charity, he made a public and solemn offering of his life to the Lord, beseeching him to accept it in satisfaction for the sins of the people. Mary Ann, who was present, was very much moved and affected at the Father's words, and being also carried away by an unusual fervour rose to her feet, and in the midst of the multitude, with few but animated words, offered her life to God, supplicating him to accept it as a holocaust for the common safety of her fellow-citizens. The Lord was pleased with the offering, and was appeased by the prayer of his beloved servant. The earthquakes immediately ceased, and the contagion decreased in proportion as Mary Ann's sickness increased, and at her death entirely disappeared.

As soon as she returned home she was assailed with a violent fever, and the dropsy, from which she had already suffered much, grew worse: and these two diseases accompanied with acute pains continued wearing her away for more than fifty-nine days. She never undressed nor took to her bed, except the last day of her life. It was a

most affecting sight to see her overwhelmed with
sufferings, and nevertheless always with a serene
countenance, and with a mind perfectly tranquil.
She would admit no relief or comfort, wishing
to die in the midst of pains for the love of her
heavenly Spouse.   That spirit of austere mortification and rigid penance, which were born, it
may be said, with her, accompanied her to the
last moment of her life.   She never eat meat,
nor took any food that was either delicate or
even substantial.   And although she was parched with an intolerable thirst, during all these
fifty-nine days she never swallowed a drop of
water.   Once she yielded to the urgent entreaties of her sister and those present who assisted
her, and took a mouthful of water, but after
keeping it a little while in her mouth she spat
it out without swallowing a drop of it.   She
was completely prostrate from the loss of
strength, but still she never laid down, but remained at one time standing, at another time
propped up on a little bed which D. Girolama
her sister had brought into her room.

When the report of her dangerous illness was
first circulated over the city, an immense number
of every rank and condition anxiously hastened
to see and speak with her for the last time.   But

the humble servant of the Lord urgently be
sought the domestics to allow no one to enter to
visit her; desiring to be alone and to keep her
mind continually fixed on God. Wherefore
they were obliged to content themselves with
coming as far as the door and making inquiries
about her. Permission, however, could not be
refused to Monsignor Fra. Pietro di Oviedo,
Bishop of Quito, who, declaring it was his duty
as pastor to visit one of his sick lambs, without
more passed on and entered her room. The
sick person at first was a little confused, and
with tender expressions of affection and humility thanked him for such condescension. But
the good prelate, when he witnessed the peace
and tranquility of her soul, which seemed already to enjoy the happiness of heaven, could
not withhold his tears; and when he was going
to take his leave he suddenly stooped and took
the invalid's hand and raised it to his lips as if
to kiss it. But Mary Ann, perceiving his intention, hastily withdrew it, and could not be pre-
vailed upon to permit it.

Her malady continuing to increase more and
more, it was judged advisable to administer to
her the holy viaticum. It was necessary to bring
it from the cathedral, which was Mary Ann's

parish: but foreseeing that it would cause a
great commotion among the people, under colour
of not giving so much trouble to the priest, she
prayed and begged so hard, that at last she succeeded in having it brought from the church of
the hospital of the poor, which was quite near
her residence.   When the priest entered the
room with the Blessed Sacrament in his hand,
although her strength was entirely gone, she
knelt down on the floor, and melting into a flood
of tender tears, received with great fervour her
Lord in the sacrament for the last time.

Three days previous to her death she lost the
entire use of her tongue, as she had desired and
asked of Almighty God.   And she herself foretold this to Petronilla of St. Bruno, her good
friend, before she took sick, who, expressing her
surprise at it, asked her in confidence the occasion of it; and Mary Ann with much simplicity
replied to her in the following terms:—"My
sister, that is not the time of discoursing about,
but of being united with God; for there is then
much to treat about with him, and it is better
to speak with God than to speak about God."
For the rest she was always self-possessed, and
retained the free and perfect use of her other
senses.   Hence it was that to ask the aid and

advice of brother Ferdinando della Croce, her
director, who never abandoned her in her last
moments, she wrote on scraps of paper what she
wished, and communicated by means of them all
that passed in the interiour of her soul. On one
of these papers she spoke thus:—"Mother St.
Catharine of Sienna came to pay me a visit, and
has shown me a most beautiful garland, with
which I will be crowned at the hour of my death:
and she told me that on Friday, between nine
and ten o'clock at night, my Spouse and his
Mother, my Mistress, the Queen of Heaven, are
to descend to take me." This same vision was
revealed, at precisely the same moment, to the
venerable mother Anna di S. Paolo, a religious
of the monastry of St. Catharine, who, in a
trance, exclaimed aloud: "Oh, this time indeed,
my sisters, our Mary Ann of Jesus is dying!"
Two religious were present at the time, who
took the liberty to ask her how she could know
it with such certainty? And she said, "I know
it because our Holy Mother St. Catharine has
come from heaven to visit Mary Ann, for the
purpose of conducting her to glory, with a most
resplendent crown destined for her triumph.

On the 25th of May, the day on which the
church celebrated the solemnity of the glorious

Ascension of Jesus Christ into heaven, she gave them to understand by her gestures, that she wished to be carried to that window of her apartment which overlooked the chapel erected in the public street to our Lady of the Angels. Here, on her knees, although on account of her extreme weakness she could scarcely support herself, she heard five successive masses. After that, being carried back into her room, she asked to write, and exposed briefly in few words her three desires. The first was that she should be transferred into the room of D. Giovanna her niece. It seemed that she would thus prepare to die dispossessed of every thing, removed from her own apartment, and upon a bed the property of another: and the more that her many instruments of penance might not be seen by the people who would come to see her. She begged in the second place, that after her death an old and worn out dress might be given her as an alms to serve as her shroud; and that her body should be buried in the church of the Society of Jesus, at the foot of the altar of our Lady of Loretto, a favour she had already solicited and obtained of the Superiours of the same Society, of which she professed herself, although unworthy, an humble daughter. Finally, she entreated her sister and niece that they would observe the greatest decency in dressing her body, and as soon as she was dead to turn her with her face towards the ground, because from her mouth a quantity of blood would flow, as in fact it happened: and she concluded by returning her most humble thanks to the household, and especially to her brother-in-law, D. Cosimo, for the good education he had given her and his kind attention to her up to that hour.

The next day she showed a desire of returning again to the window to hear the holy mass: and although the family, perhaps fearing that she would faint on account of the great prostration of her strength, hesitated for some considerable time, nevertheless, moved to pity by her urgent entreaties to be allowed her request, they were at last induced to grant it. She assisted, therefore, with much fervour at one mass, after which, not being any longer able to stand upon her feet, or to sit, she was carried back in the arms of her attendants and placed for the first time on the bed of her niece. From this they judged that her course was nearly run, and that her happy passage was near at hand. And she herself confirmed it, for hearing the bystanders speak of her death, she raised one finger of her hand, indicating in this manner, that that was to be the last day of her life. Some one present reminded her, that it would not look well for her to die before D. Cosimo, who had always been to her in place of father, and who had been summoned in haste from the villa, whither he had gone a few days before, could return home and see her alive for the last time. To this she made a sign of assent with her head; and turning her eyes from time to time around, she seemed anxiously to inquire if her brother-in-law had yet come. He arrived at last towards night, and being very much grieved to find Mary Ann reduced to the last extremity, burst into a flood of tears. But the servant of God raised her eyes and hand towards heaven, signifying to him the consolation which she felt in the thought of being speedily united to her God: after this, in the best way she could by the help of gestures, she gave him to understand that she wished to receive his blessing. D. Cosimo at first hesitated, but afterwards, seeing the invalid persist in her entreaty, he blessed her more with tears than with words.

Then Mary Ann, as if nothing now remained for her to accomplish upon earth, re-composed herself and began her agony, accompanying with the most lively sentiments of affection the extreme Unction, which in the mean time was administered to her.   FF. Luigi Vasquex, Giovanni Pietro Severino, and Alfonso Roxas, her confessors at different times, and her spiritual director brother Ferdinando della Croce, stood round her bed : and in turn suggested to her inflamed acts of divine love, which she repeated by slowly moving her lips.   She always kept the crucifix firmly claspsd in her hand and from it she never raised her eyes, except occasionally looking towards heaven with great tenderness. Whilst thus engaged, she was observed suddenly to assume a most joyful countenance, and to keep her face motionless and fixed, and her eyes rivetted on high, as if she beheld some dear object before her: after this, with the little strength that was still left her, she seemed to invite those around her to unite with her to do honour and pay their respects to the personages there present.   No one, except Br. Ferdinando della Croce, could penetrate the mystery.   He, with the paper in his hand which he had received three days before, knew immediately that her death was near at hand, and that Jesus and Mary were already come from heaven to conduct her innocent soul to glory.   Being made aware

of the fact, they all knelt down around her bed,
and one of the Fathers read the recommendation of the departing soul, according to the
ritual of the church. When this .was finished,
Father Alfonso Roxas suggested to the dying
person acts of faith, hope, and charity; after
them, taking the crucifix in his hand, he gave
her the five wounds to kiss, one after the other.
She showed plainly, by signs, that she was perfectly conscious, and accompanied every thing
with the most tender interiour affections, and
as each of the wounds was presented to her, she
impressed a sweet kiss with the little strength
which still remained. When she came to that
of the side she continued longer, shedding a
flood of sweet tears: then, as if impelled by a
transport of love, she placed her lips upon the
crown of thorns, and bending down her head,
calmly yielded up her pure spirit into the hands
of her Creator. Her precious death happened
on the 26th of May 1645, being then 26 years,
6 months, and 26 days old, on Friday, between
the hours of nine and ten at night, as she had
foretold. With respect to her features and the
appearance of her person, she was of an ordinary
stature, of a delicate constitution, and fair com-
plexion. She had a large and black eye, black

eye-brows, a broad and open forehead, her
cheeks were full and coloured, her nose small,
as well as her mouth. Her countenance, whilst
it was handsome and agreeable, so also was it
modest and amiable; and she seemed to breathe
an odour of purity and innocence. It was sufficient to look at her to feel sentiments and affections of devotion excited in the mind.

As soon as Mary Ann was dead Ferdinando
della Croce placed himself on his knees before
a little altar which had been erected in the same
room, and wishing to offer up a short prayer for
the repose of the soul departed, was immediately
bereft of his senses, and like one in an ecstacy
he continued for a full hour with his mind and
heart so absorbed in God that it was useless for
the others to call or even shake him to make
him come to himself. At last returning to himself, he rose to his feet, and with his counte
nance full of joy and serenity exclaimed—"Weep
not for the death of this happy virgin, for she
has gone straight to heaven without passing
through purgatory, and accompanied with so
many merits that she possesses many over and
above what she needs, and in which we also who
are destitute may participate here on earth."
After saying this he kissed the hands and feet

of the deceased with great reverence; and turning to the relatives he warmly recommended to them two things: The first, that they should faithfully execute her wish of being buried in the church of the Jesuits: the second, that they should use no sign of mourning, as her soul was already glorious in heaven. But there was no need of this recommendation; for no one of the family, not even her sister D. Girolama, although she wished, could shed a single tear for the death of Mary Ann. On the contrary, on the countenances of all was a visible air of tranquillity indicative of consolation and joy, as if the most fortunate accident in the world had just befallen them.

On the same night on which she died her sister with her niece, according to the direction which they had received from Mary Ann whilst alive, clothed her virginal remains in that same habit of St. Francis, which was on the skeleton, which was kept in the centre of the room: and they were induced to do this, in order to follow the custom, which was then very common throughout all the Spanish dominions. of dressing the corpse of the dead in this manner, as also because Mary Ann, to enjoy the indulgences annexed to it, had several years before, by the

advice of her confessor, worn the scapular of St.
Francis of Assisium. Besides this she had
asked before her death, that her corpse might
be dressed in an old worn out garment that
would be given her by way of alms, they judged
that they could not better comply with her wish
than by taking the above dress which was old
and worn out, and therefore well suited to show
her extreme poverty. Five chains armed with
sharp points were taken from her body, and the
sixth was left, because it was so embeded in her
sides that it could not be removed without tearing the flesh. The body remained flexible, the
countenance florid, and emitted a most odoriferous odour which soon filled the whole house. It
was placed upon a noble and rich bier, adorned
with curtains of silk, trimmed with folds and
fringe and list of gold, holding in her hand a
palm, on her head a crown, and around her was
scattered flowers of every kind, and a great
abundance of lights and torches. The hall besides exhibited nothing of grief, but was grace-
fully adorned with hangings and cloths of va-
riegated silks.

CHAPTER XVII.

THE UNIVERSAL COMMOTION OF THE CITY AT THE
REPORT OF MARY ANN'S DEATH. A LILY MIRAC-
ULOUSLY SPRINGS FROM HER BLOOD, WHENCE
SHE ACQUIRES THE TITLE OF LILY OF QUITO.
GREAT CROWDS OF PEOPLE AT THE TRANSLATION
OF HER BODY AND HER FUNERAL OBSEQUIES.
PRODIGIES WHICH TOOK PLACE BEFORE AND
AFTER IT.

At early dawn of the following day, the 27th
of May, the whole city was alive and in commotion on learning the happy death of the Blessed
Mary Ann of Jesus. The event spread like
lightning every where, and drew not only from
the houses of Quito, but from the neighbouring
villages a multitude of people, who, moving in
crowds through the streets, and crying out at
the top of their voices—*the Saint is dead, the
Saint is dead*, hurried to her late residence. To
increase the common joy and add to the universal commotion, one of the most charming and
consoling prodigies took place, by which Almighty God was pleased that very morning to
exalt the merits and publish the sanctity of his

servant. She was accustomed during her life, more for her love of suffering than for any need she had, to have herself bled at certain fixed times, every few days, and this blood, as we said before, was collected and preserved by her Indian servant in a little hole, which she had dug on purpose for it in the garden attached to the house. The same servant Catharine, having had some business or other which took her there, saw a most beautiful lily that had sprung up from the hole; and filled with wonder she ran immediately to tell the family of it. They all hastened to the spot and observed also with their own eyes the plant which had thus unexpectedly sprung forth during the night, and had already grown several palms, and was divided into three branches, at whose tops three odoriferous lilies were in full bloom. Other persons being called to see the wonder, they wished to examine every thing minutely, and removing the stone which closed the mouth of the hole, they perceived that the plant sprung from and rose out of the midst of Mary Ann's blood, which was still uncorrupt and odoriferous. They removed it with a great deal of reverence, and to their great surprise that it had roots formed as it were of little veins and delicate fibres of the same blood: and they placed it in the hand of one of the little statues of the most Blessed Virgin. And it was principally from this prodigy that the Blessed Mary Ann had from that time, and has still, the glorious title and appellation of the *Lily of Quito.*

Hardly were the doors of the hall thrown open, where the corpse of the Saint lay exposed, than a great crowd, which was already waiting, made a rush and thronged the apartment. All wished to see her, to touch her, to venerate her and to have something to keep as a relic. In a moment all the flowers which had been strewn over the corpse disappeared, and in a short time her upper garment was cut into a thousand little pieces and carried away. And some came already prepared with scissors and other tools to cut off not only her hair, but a part also of her flesh, when the relatives, to moderate somewhat their indiscreet fervour, promised to divide amongst those who wished the chains taken from off her body, which they had desired to preserve exclusively for themselves. But all they could do they were never able to satisfy the desires of the petitioners—new ones were coming in at every hour. Therefore on account of the throng of persons which was still increas-

ing, and having strong apprehensions of great
confusion, it was thought necessary to surround
the body of the deceased with armed soldiers to
protect it against the excessive and insatiate
rapacity of the pious. Before this there were
two things which took place, and which are not
to be passed over in silence. Many of those who
came, being carried away by the fervour of their
devotion, could not refrain from touching and
kissing the angelic face of the deceased; and at
the same moment that virginal face was seen to
show its disapprobation of such conduct by
swelling in such a manner as to deform itself in
appearance. The relatives perceived it, and
quickly suspecting the cause entreated the crowd
to moderate their piety, which was not at all
pleasing to Mary Ann, whose pure soul seemed
still to dread the least offence that might be
offered to her spotless body. All abstained for
the future from touching her, and her face suddenly resumed its natural beauty. What is
more, whilst they were clothing the corpse the
second time in a new dress, a profuse sweat was
observed to flow from all her limbs, and which
besides emitted a sweet fragrance. It was carefully collected in cloths which they were afterwards able to divide in many pieces, and thus

satisfy the devotion of those who also desired
something belonging to the servant of God.

There was one continued press of persons
going and returning all this and the half of the
following day, who could never satisfy themselves with gazing over and over again upon the
remains of their sainted fellow-townswoman.
Shortly after mid-day, on the 28th of May, which
fell upon Sunday, notice was given by the ring-
ing of all the bells of the city, that the body was
about to be transferred to the church of the
Jesuits: and at the same time Monsignor, the
Bishop of Quito, the chapter and clergy of the
cathedral, all the religious Orders, the judges
of the Royal Audience, the magistrates of the
province, the flower of the nobility, all splend-
idly dressed in state, and with lighted torches
in their hands, spontaneously collected and came
to do honour to the sacred function. The bier
was carried on the shoulders of priests robed in
surplice and stole; but at every little distance
they gave way to others who took their places.
The secular nobility and other more distingushed
persons came in turn and placed their bended
shoulders under the bier, from the great desire
they had of supporting in some manner that
sacred deposit. The Religious of the Society

of Jesus, the relatives of the deceased, the governor and a few more personages of distinction, together with a company of soldiers, under arms, surrounded the corpse. There was an immense crowd in the streets; and not only were the doors of the houses and shops filled with people, but the balconies, the windows and the very roofs were alive. All were eager to behold that angelic face, and to scatter clouds of flowers over her sacred corpse, and hence at first there was a murmur on all sides, then a commotion, and lastly a loud cry of exultation and joy burst forth as soon as the sacred remains were seen in the distance. To satisfy the wishes of the multitude, although the church of the Jesuits was quite near the residence of Mary Ann, it was necessary to make a long circuit and proceed slowly through the principal streets of the city, all lined with people who were unable to remain stationary, on account of the unusual prodigy which they had continually before them; for wherever the procession approached the air was sensibly filled with a delicious fragrance which issued from the corpse of the Saint, which, after more than thirty hours, continued not only as fresh and blooming as when alive, but diffused an agreeable odour which inundated the soul with spiritual consolation.

The festival of our Lady of Loretto had been celebrated that day in the church of the Jesuits, and her statue was conspicuously exposed above the main altar. The vast temple was adorned all over with tapestry; the walls were covered with festoons, garlands, and rich silks, so that it seemed more like a triumphal procession than a funeral, to judge from the magnificence of the preparation and the confused murmur of the dense mass. What served to increase the tumult was, that the bier was hardly within the portals of the church, before the corpse of the deceased was distinctly observed to open one of its eyes, and a few minutes later, when it reached the centre and was deposited opposite the high altar, it was again observed clearly and distinctly to open the other also, and to fix its sight upon the statue of the most Blessed Virgin. There was then a great commotion amongst the people, and a general rush was made towards the bier, every one being eager to behold the prodigy with his own eyes. And great confusion would most certainly have ensued, had not Father Alfonso Roxas, in order to calm the noise and soothe the general commotion, mounted a bench, and raising up the head of Mary Ann, showed to the multitude the eyes wide open and full of life, and then closed them again with his own hands.

After the agitation had somewhat subsided, they began to sing the solemn office of requiem; but it was found impossible to proceed with it, on account of the continued acclamations of the people and the great press of the multitude, who, after forcing every barrier, and cutting in pieces the third dress with which the sacred remains had been covered, were prepared with instruments to cut off the fingers of the hands. The singing, therefore, having been interrupted, and prayers and threats being insufficient to restrain the devotion of the populace within proper bounds, by order of Monsignor the Bishop and the dignitaries of the city, the corpse was placed in a wooden coffin and consigned to the care of the Jesuits, who buried it immediately under ground in the chapel of St. Joseph, the other grave not being yet ready, which was being prepared at the foot of the altar of the most Blessed Virgin of Loretto, as Mary Ann had arranged before her death. A month later the solemn obsequies were again renewed in the same church at the city's expense, at which a noisy concourse of persons assisted; and Father

Alfonso Roxas read a long panegyric in honour
of the deceased, which was afterwards published.
When the service was over and the people dis-
persed, Monsignor the Bishop, with the Presi-
dent of the Royal Audience, went to the chapel
of St. Joseph, where the servant of God had
been interred, and, having opened the coffin,
they found the body still whole and uncorrupted.
The coffin was again closed and sealed, and
carried in a private procession to the chapel of
our Blessed Lady of Loretto, and deposited in
the new tomb. Three years later it was again
opened and the body was found decomposed, as
Mary Ann had desired and asked; but it emitted
a delicious odour, which filled the whole church.
They collected the precious bones, and with
much reverence replaced them in a leaden coffin
which bore the following simple inscription:

HERE LIES THE ANGELIC VIRGIN

MARY ANN OF JESUS Y PAREDES.

But the fame of her wonderful life, and the
odour of her heroic virtues were not buried
with her body in the earth, but remain still
living in the remembrance of all in South
America, and were also appreciated in other
parts of the Catholic world, where many like-

nesses of the saint are to be found, taken immediately after her death and drawn to life.

CHAPTER XVIII.

THE ESTEEM AND THE UNIVERSAL OPINION OF SANCTITY IN WHICH THE BLESSED MARY ANN WAS HELD. AUTHENTIC TESTIMONIES OF HER CONFESSORS.

I could make a long enumeration of the testimonies of those who deposed in the different processes, to the esteem and universal opinion of sanctity in which the Blessed Mary Ann was held both before and after her death. Although she led a hidden and solitary life, nevertheless her innocence and austerity were things so out of the usual course, that they could not be kept concealed from the eyes of the public. Hence the name of saint by which she was generally called; and those titles of angelic virgin, spotless soul, pure lily, which were given her by every class of persons. Not only in the city of Quito, but also in the other provinces, and in every part of South America, she enjoyed the reputation and opinion of superior sanctity: and I find that many personages of distinguished nobility came from distant provinces to Quito, that they might have the consolation of seeing and becoming acquainted with her.

But to prove what has been asserted, I think I cannot do better than transcribe here the attestations of her confessors, who were for many years her spiritual directors and knew her intimately. Father Luigi Vasquez, a man who was naturally extremely cautious in giving an opinion, made no difficulty to affirm, "that the sanctity of Mary Ann bore, according to his judgment, a most striking resemblance to that of St. Catharine of Sienna." Father Gio. Pietro Severino was of the same opinion. He was professor of Theology in the University of St. Gregory in Quito, and on the 27th of May, hearing the signal given by the bell that Mary Ann, who had been his penitent, was dead, he interrupted his lecture, and after pronouncing before his scholars the highest encomiums on the virtues of the deceased, concluded thus his discourse: "In my judgment the degree of sanctity of our Blessed Mary Ann of Jesus is not less than that of St. Catharine of Sienna, whom she proposed to imitate in every thing."

Father John Camaccio, when he first heard of Mary Ann's death, wrote to Captain D. Co-

simo, her brother-in-law, a letter which was
afterwards cited at length in the process, and is
to the following effect: "I know not whether I
ought to condole or rejoice with you at the news
which I have just received. I deeply feel that
a person of such distinguished sanctity is no
more. I console myself by the certainty which
I have of the singular glory which she enjoys in
heaven, and in having been also the instrument,
although unworthy, which the Lord made use
of to advance her to that high degree of virtue,
to give a detailed account of which would require more time and more space than a letter
will permit. Passing over, therefore, in silence
whatever regards the exteriour appearance of
Mary Ann, which was visible to every one, and
confining myself to a brief sketch of her interiour, which may serve as material for the discourse which you are planning, I will say, in the
first place, that our Lord raised her to the highest degree of contemplation, which consists in
knowing God and his perfections without long
discourses, and loving him without interruption.
Her penances at the time when I directed her
were certainly extraordinary, and far above
what such a frail body would seem capable of
enduring; and these I permitted her after much

reflection and consideration, because I was convinced that they had been inspired by Almighty
God. She was in the habit of carrying upon her
person, at the same time, six or seven rough
chains, many times during the day disciplined
herself to blood, spent many nights fastened to
a cross, and many extended upon a ladder. Her
fasts were without doubt extraordinary; for besides those on bread and water alone, which she
frequently practised in the beginning; for the
space of several years she never eat any thing
except every fifteen days, and then her food
consisted of a thin slice of bread which she
afterwards soon threw up again. She had made
a vow of chastity and virginity which she observed without a blemish, or the least thought
that could tarnish it. She made also a vow of
obedience to her confessor, which she kept with
the greatest exactness, and another of poverty,
by which she divested herself of every thing,
even to the keys of her trinkets, neither giving
nor receiving any thing without the permission
of her confessor. She passed the greater portion of the day and night in vocal or mental
prayer, in examens, spiritual reading and contemplation, giving scarcely an hour to sleep.
She had such a singular purity of conscience

that it was necessary for absolution to have recourse to something of her past life, as she never brought any matter for absolution. She was extremely humble and keenly felt that others should regard her as virtuous, and to avoid observation she always sought the most retired corners of the church. She asked of our Lord that he would not conduct her by the way of favours and consolations, but rather by that of hardships and adversities, in imitation of D. Maria Vela, to whom she was very much devoted, and whose life she constantly read to copy it in herself; and she was so successful in her prayer that the tedium, the desolations and the interiour agonies which she suffered would have long before caused her death if the Lord had not, as I judge, miraculously preserved her life to increase her merit; and in her desolation what afflicted her most was the fear of giving trouble to others, or of seeming peevish in her answers. I could extend this relation much farther, but this letter will answer your purpose."

Still more diffuse is the juridical testimony, which Father Antonio Monosalvas, another of Mary Ann's confessors, gave in the first information taken in 1670. And since many of the facts which are deposed are already related in

other places, I will content myself with only
adding a few things here in his own words.
"The life," said he, "of the venerable Mary
Ann of Jesus, was extraordinary and singular
as regarded the penances, the fasts, and the
mortifications which she performed.   The deponent saw a hair shirt, made something like
an Indian's under dress, which fitted tight to
the body, and came down to the girdle, and with
sleeves to the elbows, and studded over with
sharp pointed steel.   This hair cloth was woven
of hair so rough, that the deponent attests that
as soon as he saw it his flesh began to shudder.
And the deponent knows these things from having been the spiritual father of the venerable
servant of God for the space of six or seven
years, a little more or less, at which time she
communicated what he has deposed and what he
will presently depose. . . . .   During the
whole course of her earthly career she preserved
the first grace which she had received in bap-
tism ; and she never sinned mortally or committed a deliberate venial sin : and any imper-
fections which she perhaps had, were involuntary
and without deliberation. . . . . .   Her
chastity was angelic,—she never confessed any

thing that cast a shade of blemish against
this virtue. She was naturally of a meek disposition and knew not what it was to become
angry. The fervour and devotion which she
had when she communicated, were so great that
many times the deponent did not know her,
because her face became as it were that of an
angel. Whenever she fixed her eyes upon the
most Blessed Sacrament, she renewed her three
vows of chastity, poverty, and obedience. The
first years of her life she exercised herself in
fervorous prayers, giving at least two hours to it
every day, one in the morning and the other in
the evening. Our Lord afterwards raised her
to such a lofty contemplation, and so close a
union with her beloved Spouse, that she never
lost sight of the divine presence, and had no
more need of books to find matter for contemplation; for whatever she saw or heard supplied
her with abundant material for entertaining herself whole days and entire nights in praising
and loving her heavenly Spouse. In contemplating the mysteries of the passion of Jesus
Christ her heart melted with love; and here it
was that her soul experienced the greatest consolations and delights. . . . . . She was

venerated and regarded as a living saint every
where in the city; and she was designated by
all by no other name than that of saint; and
when parents desired any great blessing for
their daughters they were accustomed to say:—
'May it please God that our children be like
the saint,' meaning Mary Ann of Jesus."

Father Luca della Cueva, as well as Father
Alfonso Roxas, left in writing the fullest testimonies of Máry Ann's virtues; the first in a
manuscript which he sent from his missions
among the infidels to Quito, that it might be
inserted in the process; the other in a long discourse which he read when the obsequies were
performed the second time. I shall say nothing
of Brother Ferdinando della Croce, having
already had frequent occasions to mention him
in the course of this history.

CHAPTER XIX.

NUMEROUS PRODIGIES WROUGHT BY ALMIGHTY
GOD THROUGH THE INTERCESSION OF THE
BLESSED MARY ANN. A FEW OF THE MOST
REMARKABLE ONES ARE GIVEN. CONVERSIONS
AND REFORMATION OF LIVES PRODUCED BY
THE READING OF HER LIFE.

But were the testimonies of men wanting, that of the Almighty would certainly be sufficient, who, by many and stupendous miracles, manifested his approbation of the sanctity and precious death of his faithful servant. We will relate a few of them for the purpose of exciting the devotion of the faithful to implore her assistance and intercession.

And first of all, the rooms where the Blessed Mary Ann had dwelt were frequently seen at night illuminated with a bright light; and a sweet smell of lilies was perceived for several years over the whole apartment which she formerly occupied. At the report of this prodigy many persons from without obtained entrance into the building, which had been converted

into a monastery, and judges were sent to take
juridical information of the fact: and all
agreed that the cause was supernatural and
miraculous, as not a plant or a branch of such
a flower was to be found in the house. Likewise from the hole where Mary Ann's blood had
been preserved for so many years, the most
odoriferous lilies would frequently shoot forth,
and around them other flowers of wonderful
beauty, although the ground had never been
cultivated, neither had any plants of the kind
ever been sown in the whole garden.

The Indian, Catharine, whom we have so frequently mentioned in this history, dwelt near
the residence of the servant of God. She was
weighed down with years, and had almost entirely lost the sense of hearing. She attested
in the process that many nights, when at her
prayers, she heard a harmonious concert of angelic voices issuing from the chamber of her
former mistress, and that among them she could
easily distinguish that of D. Sebastiana di
Casso, and high above them all that of the
Blessed Mary Ann, which was heard above all
the rest. And this alone cured her of her
deafness.

Whilst D. Marta Rodriguez Paredes, niece of the servant of God, was spending some days at one of her villas in the country, a poor miserable woman of the place was suffering dreadfully from an acute pain in the head, which gave her no rest. Her mistress, moved to pity at the sight of the convulsions of the poor creature, to whom all human remedies were of no assistance, applied to her forehead a very small piece of the bone of the Saint, tying it up in a bandage that had also been stained with her blood; and the night being far advanced, the good Lady retired to take some repose. The young woman, although she was suffering dreadfully, did not hesitate to admit even that night a guilty manservant with whom she had had criminal intercourse: but he had hardly entered before the two wretches saw, to their great terror, the roof of the house open, and a most beautiful young Lady, with a majestic countenance, descend from heaven, with a rod of fire in her hand, and attended by four young men with torches in their hands. The heavenly young Lady approached the place of iniquity, and looking at the guilty woman with eyes flashing fire: "*How is it possible,*" said she, "*that you could go so far in*

24

your impudence as to keep my relics about your person? Either remove them immediately, or if you do not I take your life with this rod of fire." Full of terror the guilty woman quickly threw the relics of Mary Ann far away from her, and at the same moment the vision disappeared. Both the guilty wretches remained for more than two hours so oppressed by terror that they had not the strength to move a single step, and all they could do was to ask by loud cries pardon of God and the assistance of men. The domestics were aroused by their cries, and from the mouth of the guilty pair learnt the fact which was confirmed by the prodigy of their having remained thus motionless for many hours; and both, after having made a good confession, asked and obtained leave to be married the very day after the apparition just mentioned

Word was brought to D. Girolama de Paredes, sister of Mary Ann, that D. Maria di Casso, her daughter and wife of D. Alfonso Sanchez de Luna, was at a house in the country, and in great danger of her life. Although the hour was late at night, D. Girolama mounted a mule and started to visit her sick daughter, and whilst journeying on she poured forth fervent prayers to her sainted sister to succour her daughter D. Maria. Her prayer was hardly finished before a sweet sleep overpowered D. Girolama whilst she was riding her mule, and Mary Ann appeared to her and addressed her in the words: "*Sister*," said she, "*you seek an impossibility of me, for the death of your daughter is already decreed, and it is but right ;*" and the vision immediately disappeared. The good Lady then awoke, and bowing to the adorable dispensations of Almighty God, was so fully persuaded that her daughter would die, that when arrived at the villa where the sick person was, to all who endeavoured to animate her to hope that her daughter would recover, she replied that her death was certain, as Mary Ann had told her so: as in fact it turned out, for D. Maria died within a few days.

D. Girolama experienced the help of her sister more favourably inclined towards herself in many accidents, but more especially in two grievous infirmities. The first was when her breast was attacked with five cancers, all at the same time, and attended with horrible pains, which were fast hastening her to the grave. In this extremity the sick person applied to the

affected parts a cloth saturated with the blood
which Mary Ann had discharged from her mouth
after her death, and begged her that she would
succour her as she had succoured so many other
sick persons who had recourse to her intercession. The termination of D. Girolama's prayer
and her instantaneous cure took place at the
same precise moment. The other sickness from
which she was evidently cured by the prayers
of her sainted sister, was a malignant fever, on
account of which she was given over by the physicians. She applied to her person one of the
under-dresses belonging to her sister, and at the
touch of the relic the fever suddenly abated
with a notable change in the invalid for the
better, and in a few days she was perfectly
cured.

By the application of some relic belonging to
Mary Ann, the mother of Maria Vilchez and
Father Ignazio Cazeres were miraculously cured
of violent fevers, as also a poor Indian, to whom
Tommaso Paredes, brother of the Saint, gave a
small particle of her clotted blood to drink in a
glass of water.

For the cure of D. Giuseppa d'Escorza of a
violent malignant fever, nothing more was re-

quired than to look at the picture of the servant
of God; for no sooner was it brought into the
invalid's chamber than the fever immediately
diminished, and in a few days she was perfectly
well.

D. Luigi Troia D. D., a canon of the cathedral and the vicar of the Bishop of Quito, was
despaired of by the physicians, and after receiving the last sacraments disposed himself for
death. Brother Ferdinando della Croce paid
him a visit, and seeing the state of the sick
person, sent for a picture of Mary Ann, and
when the image was brought he exhorted the
sick man to have recourse to her intercession.
He did so with much confidence; and putting
the picture on his head he grew considerably
better at the same moment, and continued to
improve till he was entirely cured, and survived
many years.

In the villa d'Ybarra a poor Indian woman
was suffering very much from a disease of the
heart, for which there was no human remedy to
be found. She applied with confidence to her
breast a picture of Mary Ann, and for the rest
of her life was perfectly free of that troublesome disease.

D. Francesca di Carvial suffered from tumours
in the face, which, besides disfiguring her,
caused her acute pains.   D. Girolama de
Paredes, niece of the servant of God, could
find no remedy for a strange swelling of the
whole right hand.   Another virtuous young
lady called Emmanuela Infausti, was tormented
in the knee by a hard fleshy crescence, much
bigger than an egg.   Two Indians, one named
Angiolina and the other Catharine Paredes,
were unable to move an arm, the first from a
violent contraction of the nerves, the other on
account of an incurable tumour, according to
the judgment of physicians.   And finally, D.
Francesco Aureliano had a sore on his back
from his twelfth year, which could never be
healed.   All these, by merely bandaging on
the parts affected some relic, either of the
chains or the clothes of the saint, in a short
time were free and cured of every disorder
without any sign of the former disease.

D. Francesca Azevedo, seeing a little girl of
six years of age horribly deformed with the
scrofula in the throat, bandaged the neck of
the innocent little creature with one of the
ribbons that had been used to adorn the coffin

of Mary Ann, and at the end of four days the
little girl was perfectly cured of the evil.

D. Emmanuele Guerrero de Salazar, nephew
of the servant of God, was returning to Quito
from the villa of Ybarra, and carried suspended
from his neck a little picture of his aunt,
painted upon a tablet, which he had copied
himself, because, as the picture resembled her
very much, many desired to have copies taken
from it.   Guerrero was travelling along in
company with Captain Diego Migno, and one
of his attendants; and all three were discoursing on the road of the virtues of Mary Ann,
and of the wonders performed by Almighty
God through her intercession.   Meanwhile D.
Emmanuele being come to a torrent, in the
attempt to cross it, his beast made an unfortunate slip and pitched him head-foremost into
the water, and, to add to his misfortune, the
animal fell upon him with the whole weight of
its body.   His companions could render him no
assistance, for, besides the danger of falling
themselves if they approached the current, the
place was so filled with rocks that there was no
possibility of dismounting from their saddles.
In this imminent danger no other resource was

left him than to invoke the aid of his aunt, who was not deaf to his supplication. It was perhaps half an hour that D. Emmanuele remained with his head under water, and with the weight of the beast upon him, which was crushing him, when good luck would have it, some Indians passed by and extracted Guerrero from under the mule, and afterwards lifted him up from out of the water, not dead, as might have reasonably been expected, but sound and not in the least hurt, and with Mary Ann's picture besides unsoiled and untouched. After thanking his kind preserver with all the affection of his heart, as may easily be imagined, they all three resumed their journey and arrived at the country called Guaygliabamba, where they halted to pass the night. Whether it was fright on account of the danger he had just escaped, or originated from some other cause Guerrero was attacked that same night with a violent dysentery, of which he thought he would have died: imploring however a second time the intercession of his aunt, he found himself suddenly rid of his complaint and able to continue his journey the next morning to Quito.

D. Marta Rodriguez de Paredes being one

day in the sugar-house belonging to her parents, the hour being about noon, when the sun was shining and the heavens perfectly clear, saw that the kitchen of the house was on fire, in which a Moorish slave was sleeping. Knowing the danger of a conflagration, which would be increased by the blowing of the wind, D. Marta and D. Alfonso, her brother, ran to give assistance and prevent the fire from spreading; but they soon saw that all human means would be ineffectual to check it, and that without doubt it would extend to the house and the adjoining building, and after that reach and destroy the crop of sugar cane, to the serious loss of its owners. In this perplexity D. Marta remembered that she had in her room where she slept a picture of Mary Ann, and going after it immediately she brought it into the yard of the house, and with great confidence pressing the image in her arms: "*Aunt*," said she, "*how can you allow this little country house of ours to be burnt up?*" and after she had said this she approached the flames and held the picture before them. Something like little drops of sweat were observed on the face of the picture, occasioned by its being brought in close contact with the

raging element; and after this the sky which
had been perfectly clear became suddenly dark-
ened, and such a violent rain fell that the fire
was totally extinguished, the Moor saved, all
the furniture of the house unharmed, and only
the kitchen, where the fire originated, was partly
destroyed without any other damages, which at
one time seemed imminent.

Diego Calahorrano, when crossing the Lata-
cunga, a rapid and deep river, was carried away
by the current, and was in imminent danger of
being drowned. He had recourse in his danger
to the servant of God, a small particle of whose
dress he carried about with him as a relic, and
without knowing how, he found himself on the
bank of the river, rescued from the water and
consequently from death.

D. Basilia Olmos was very much troubled
with a growing tumour in her left breast, and
which was pronounced incurable by human art.
A few of the hairs of Mary Ann were given to
D. Basilia as a relic, that she might apply them
to the part affected; but she in place of using
them for the purpose for which they were given
her, put them away in a casket. For three successive nights she heard a voice in her sleep

that invited her to apply the aforesaid relic, but
thinking it was wrong to give any credence to
dreams, she did not obey. One day whilst
making her confession to Monsignor Salvatore
Bermudez, Bishop of La Pace, and Archbishop
elect of La Plata, the prelate spoke to her of
her sufferings, and advised her to recommend
herself with confidence to the servant of God, to
promise an alms in her name, and lastly to apply
to the affected part a relic of her. D. Basilia
was surprised to hear the prelate speak in this
manner, and frankly told him of the voice she
had heard for three successive nights; then
without further hesitation, as soon as she was
returned home, she placed the Saint's hair upon
the tumour, and in an instant, at the very touch,
the evil disappeared and she was perfectly cured.
The prodigy was known all over the city, and
several persons wishing that she should testify,
under oath, to the fact in the juridical process,
the Lady made much difficulty about taking the
requisite oath. The day at length appointed
for taking authentic information of the prodigy
that had happened to her arrived, and therefore
becoming more timorous than ever, she absolutely refused to give her evidence. This re-

fusal was certainly very untimely, and God, who
wished his servant glorified, caused a sharp pain
to strike D. Basilia in the left breast, by which
being overcome she began, of her own accord,
to cry out that she would take the oath without
further difficulty; and then the pain, which was
only sent her again for this end, instantaneously
disappeared, and she never after felt the least
symptom of it.

It would really be an endless task to gather
together, without omitting one, all the prodigies
operated either by touching the relics or the
pictures of Mary Ann of Jesus, by the invoca-
tion of her name or by simply promising to con-
cur in some manner to promote her honour.   A
great many of these miraculous events may be
read duly authenticated in the different processes; and in an especial manner she has shown
herself in AMERICA the particular patroness of
woman in labour, many of whom she has rescued
in a most singular manner from imminent danger
of perishing, together with their offspring.

Finally, the reading of Mary Ann's life alone
was the cause of the conversion of many obstinate sinners, and an improvement in the lives
of others.   Not to tire the reader's patience, I

will only relate here one single instance. There
lived in the city of Quaiaquil, in South America,
a young lady descended of a noble family, whose
name was Catharine. Her manners were in
other respects innocent, but very gay and very
sprightly; and perhaps in danger of falling and
losing herself on account of her excessive indul-
gence in setting off her person and in vain ornaments, which foolishly occupied her the best
portion of the day. On one occasion being on
a visit with her mother to the house of some
relatives, she heard the company speak of the
wonderful virtues of Mary Ann, and above all,
of the extraordinary effects which an attentive
reading of her life produced in every class of
persons. These things appeared to the young
lady mere exaggerations of minds inclined to be
too credulous; and with an air of contempt she
said she would like to read Mary Ann's life to
see if it would operate those great wonders in
her, which they reported at so cheap a rate.
She began, therefore, from mere curiosity, to
run over with her eyes the history of her life
that had fallen into her hands; and after reading over a good portion she went on boasting
that she felt no change in herself for the better,

25

and laughed at the credulity of others. She
came at last to that chapter where it is related
how the servant of God, a little child of seven
years, when in the country, was found on her
knees in the woods, scourging her innocent body
at the same time with a bundle of thorny herbs:
and here it was that God had resolved to con-
vince and convert her; for Catharine, at the
recital of this, entered into herself, and compar-
ing her vanity and delicacy with the penance
and austerity of that little innocent child, broke
forth into a flood of bitter tears for her past
folly; after this, stripping herself of every vain
ornament, she laid aside her rich and showy
clothes which she had on, and to the great wonder of the whole city, appeared in the humble
dress of the third Order of St. Dominic. Not
even satisfied with this, she entreated her relatives, and succeeded at last in being brought to
Quito, where, in the monastery of St. Catharine
of Sienna, she took the religious habit, and cor-
responding to the prodigy operated in her by
reading the life of Mary Ann of Jesus, she lived
and died in the odour of no ordinary virtue.

And this is precisely the fruit which, with
the help of God and the intercession of the

Blessed Mary Ann, I promise myself from my slender exertions. I shall look upon myself as well repaid if this history edify and becomes the means of salvation to many, who come with minds well disposed to peruse it.

CHAPTER XX.

TWO MIRACLES APPROVED OF BY THE SACRED CONGREGATION OF RITES BEFORE THE BEATIFICATION OF THE SERVANT OF GOD.

ANGELA POLIDO ESCORZA, a noble matron of the city of Quito, was in November of 1760 suddenly assailed with acute pains in her bowels: after this her stomach began to swell in a strange manner. Her physicians at first pronounced it an effect of pregnancy, but after nine months and more had passed, and the swelling still increasing with the pains, they suspected that it was some very serious internal disease. Nor was it long before it began to manifest itself with dangerous and mortal symptoms, such as frequent discharges of blood, palpitation of the heart, nervousness, acute pains and spasms,

difficulty in breathing, and continual danger of
suffocation. The invalid found no rest by day
or night, and she was unable to move herself
without the greatest pain and difficulty. She
continued in this state for twenty-two months,
and having now been given over by her physicians, and from prostration of strength reduced
to the last extremity, she ordered every description of medicine to be removed from her room,
and sent for Father Domenico Coleti, of the
Society of Jesus, to whom she wished to make
her general confession, and so prepare herself
for death. A short time after she received the
holy viaticum and extreme unction with sentiments of much devotion. Whilst they were re-
citing the last prayers for the recommendation
of the departing soul, raising her eyes she saw
an image of the venerable Mary Ann, which was
suspended on the wall opposite to her bed, and
at the same time she felt a rising in her heart
of a firm confidence of obtaining a cure through
the intercession of the servant of God, for whose
sake she had already promised to give five piasters of silver. She sent to get a small particle
of her bone, which she kept as a relic, and di-
viding it into two parts: "*O most glorious*

Saint," said she, "*and my fellow-countrywoman,
born in Quito like myself, ah, why do you permit
me to suffer such pains without the least relief?
I promise you, in case I am cured, to make a
novena, and to pay the five piasters which I have
promised.*" Having said this, she swallowed a
piece of the bone, and with the other made the
sign of the cross over her stomach. At this
moment D. Giuseppa Castello entered the room,
and fixing her eyes upon the invalid, in her
astonishment she cried aloud: "*O, my Angiola,
what has become of your disease?*" At these
words the invalid, as if coming to herself, ran
her hand over her stomach, which she found in
its natural state. The pains were all gone, all
bad symptoms had disappeared, and sound and
vigorous she rose and sat up in her bed; then
hastily dressing herself she ran below to call
the servant-maids, who were lamenting in their
own apartment the approaching death of their
mistress; she assembled her friends and neighbours, and with great jubilee related to them
her miraculous cure. The whole city was full
of it, and they gave public thanks to Almighty
God, amidst a great concourse of people.

D. Angiola enjoyed perfect health for the

25*

next twelve years; but in 1771 she was tried
by Almighty God with a new and dangerous
sickness. She felt a great swelling in her
womb, which in a short time became so big
that she was scarcely able to move. D.
Giuseppe Rosario, a celebrated physician, was
called in haste. who, after making his observations, pronounced the origin of the disease to
be two internal scirrhus—substances of extraordinary size, which were incurable, on account
of the difficulty of applying suitable remedies.
The pious lady wished to receive the last
sacraments and make her confession to D. Giovanni Ignazio de Aquilar, the parish priest, who
exhorted her to have recourse to the venerable
Mary Ann, and ask of her the grace of a second
cure. The lady followed his advice; and all
that day, which was the 10th of February 1772,
she held an image of the saint pressed to her
bosom. The next day she wished to go to the
church, to receive holy communion, and was
little less than carried thither loaded with
pains. She had scarcely received the body of
our Lord, when she heard an interiour voice,
which said to her that *the grace desired had
been granted her.* And so in fact it was; for,

getting upon her feet, she quickly descended
the steps of the altar by herself, and having
come to the centre of the church she cried out
in a loud voice, "*A miracle.*" She heard mass,
kneeling, and returned home attended by a
great crowd, perfectly cured. Of these two
miracles there can be no doubt, on account of
the nature of the diseases, as well as on account
of the multitude of witnesses, and above all on
account of the decree of the Sovereign Pontiff,
by which both of them have been approved.

CHAPTER XXI.

INTRODUCTION OF THE CAUSE INTO THE SACRED
CONGREGATION OF RITES. ITS PROGRESS AND
TERMINATION.

On account of the numerous prodigies which
Almighty God wrought in every part of South
America at the intercession of the venerable
Mary Ann of Jesus, the citizens of Quito, and
especially the relatives of the servant of God,
made humble supplication to Monsignor the

Bishop, that he would by authority take juridical testimony in regard to her life, virtues,
and miracles. The first initiatory steps, therefore, were commenced in 1670 by Monsignor
Alfonso della Pegna, and in the course of eight
years a great number of witnesses, most of
them ocular, were examined in due form and
with much care. D. Giovanni Guerrero di
Salazar, nephew of Mary Ann, was to have
carried the authenticated copy to Rome; but
the ship in which he sailed was overtaken by a
furious tempest near the port of Havana and
wrecked, and all was lost except the passengers.
A second expedition undertaken in 1706 succeeded no better; for the ship which carried
the acts fell into the power of the enemies of
Spain, who pillaged these seas. The citizens
of Quito did not however desist from promoting the cause of the beatification of their
fellow-townswoman, and in 1751 they despatch-
ed a third copy of the process, which in 1754
finally reached Rome. The validity of it
having been discussed and approved of, the
formal introduction of the cause was proposed
in the Sacred Congregation of Rites, which
was admitted and signed on the 17th of De-

cember, 1757, by the Sovereign Pontiff, Bene-
dict XIV.

The next year letters in due form were ex-
pedited to the Bishop of Quito to begin the
process or examination, authorized by the Pope,
with regard to the general estimation in which
she was held; and at the same time other
letters of the same kind for the formation of
the process, with respect to her virtues and
miracles in particular, taking the testimony of
those who, from their advanced age, were
likely to die soon. All these processes being
come to Rome, and with them the canon D.
Giovanni del Castillo, sent expressly by the
city of Quito to solicit and promote the cause,
the question of her virtues was proposed in
three distinct Congregations, and at last the
Sovereign Pontiff, Pius VI., solemnly approved
and declared them heroic.

Owing to the vicissitudes of the times which
occurred under the two Pontiffs, Pius VI. and
VII., the cause proceeded no further, and only
in these last years it was resumed by the care
of the Reverend Father John Roothaan, General of the Society of Jesus, to whom its pro-
motion was confided by the Bishop and the city
of Quito. And it was but just that the Society

should take an interest in promoting the glory of one who had been as it were intimately connected with it.

Two miracles were then proposed to be discussed, and after having been thoroughly sifted in all due forms, in three Congregations, his Holiness, Pope Pius IX., approved them on the 11th of January, 1847, and on the 29th of September, 1850, declared that they might safely proceed to the solemn beatification, which afterwards took place in the Vatican Basilic, on the 10th day of November of the year 1853, in presence of their Eminences the Cardinals belonging to the sacred Congregation of Rites, the Consultors of the same, the Chapter, and Vatican Seminary.   Reverend Father Peter Beckx, General of the Society of Jesus, presented himself before his Eminence Cardinal Patrizi, begging him that he would deign to order the publication of the Apostolic Brief; this favour being granted and the Brief read, the image of the beatified was immediately uncovered, amid the festive sounds of the sacred bells and the discharge of artillery; and after singing the Ambrosian Hymn, a solemn pontifical mass, with splendid music, was intoned by Monsignor Bighi, Archbishop of Filippi, and Vicar of the Vatican Chapter. At half-past three in the afternoon his Holiness descended from his Vatican residence to the august Basilic, accompanied by the sacred College and his noble court, to venerate the newly beatified saint.

The solemn beatification of the Blessed Mary Ann of Jesus would have taken place much sooner, if the disturbances occasioned by internal dissensions and party strifes in Quito had not prevented it. Let us hope nevertheless, that the newly beatified saint will look down from heaven with a propitious eye upon her country, restore peace and tranquility to it, and above all preserve it from the assaults and snares of the enemies of Religion and the Catholic Church.

DEO GRATIAS ET MARIÆ ET MARIANNÆ.

INSCRIPTIONS

Affixed in the Vatican Basilic at the solemn
Beatification of the Venerable Servant of God.

I.

MARIANNAE. DE. PAREDES. ET. FLOREI. VIRGINI.

QVAE. ET. QVITI. LILIVNI. DICTA. EST.

PIVS. PAPA. IX. PONT. MAX.

MINORES. CAELITVM. HONORES.

XII. KAL. DEC. ANN. REP. SAL. MDCCCLIII.

DECERNIT.

II.

JOANNAM. SANGVERA.

SACERDOTI. OPERANTI. ADSTANTEM.

MARITVS. POCIONE. DISTRICTO.

IN. TEMPLVM. INVADIT.

CONFVGIT. JOANNA. IN. SINVM.

B. MARIANNÆ. ILLIC. ADORANTIS.
QVÆ. IRAM. FORENTIS. MARITI. FRANGIT
AGNOQVE. MANSVETIOREM. REDDIT.

III.

ERO. QVASI. ROS. ISRAEL.
GERMINABIT. SICVT. LILIVM.
ET. ERVMPET. RADIX. EJOS. VT. LIBANI.
LAETABITVR. DESERTA. ET. INVIA.
ET. EXVLTABIT. SOLITVDO.
ET. FLOREBIT. QVASI. LIBIVM.

IV.

ANGELAM. POLIDO. A. DVPLICI. LETHALI. MORBO.
EX. IMPROVISO. INCOLVMEM.
JOSEPHVS. CASTELLO. MIRATOR.
PRODIGVQVE. AVCTOREM. QVÆERIT.
B. MARIANNAE. IMAGINEM. ET. OS.
CVJVS. PARTEM. DEGLVTIERAT.
ANGELA. OSTENDIT.
26

V.

POST. ANNOS. XII. EADEM. ANGELA.

DVPLICI. SCIRRHOMATE. AD. MORTEM.

CERTO. TRAHITVR.

B. MARIANNAM. ANGELA. ADVOCAT.

SESEQVE. AD. TEMPLVM. DEFERRI. IVBET

CAELESTI. PASCITVR. CONVIVIO.

EX. IMPROVISO. ITERVM.

INCOLVMITATEM. RECVPERAT.

THE END.

Lightning Source UK Ltd.
Milton Keynes UK
UKHW021841020622
403916UK00003B/175